16.6.06

University of
Chester

CHESTER CAMPUS
LIBRARY
01244 513301

This book is to be returned on or before the last date stamped below. Overdue charges will be incurred by the late return of books.

Young minds in our schools

a guide for teachers and others working in schools

by Peter Wilson
drawings by Christine Roche

YoungMinds
for children's mental health

YoungMinds Publications

Published by YoungMinds,
the children's mental health charity,
102-108 Clerkenwell Road, London EC1M 5SA

www.youngminds.org.uk

First published 2003
Reprinted with some additions 2004
Copyright ©YoungMinds 2003

The rights of Peter Wilson and Christine Roche to be identified as
the author and illustrator of the work have been asserted by them
in accordance with the Copyright, Designs and Patents Act 1988.

Drawings copyright ©Christine Roche 2003

Printed in England by BSC Print, London

British Library Cataloguing in Publication Data
A CIP catalogue record for this book is available from
the British Library

ISBN 0-9545123-5-9

*To my wife Jil and children
Emma, Sam and Jessica and
all those at YoungMinds who have
kept my mind young*

Acknowledgements

In writing this book, I have benefited from the knowledge and experience of Jeanni Barlow, freelance educational consultant and trainer. I am most grateful for the encouragement and advice she has given me.

I have also gained a great deal from a wide range of colleagues and practitioners in YoungMinds in the fields of education and mental health.

I must also give special thanks to Manju Chadee, Kate Cherniavsky, Tarryn Hawley, Jane Jacobson, Paula Lavis, Imogen Le Patourel and Kelly Porter who have helped me make sense of what I am writing and to Richard Meier for actually putting the book together in such a creative and presentable form.

I am very appreciative of Christine Roche's drawings which give such breadth and humour to the book.

Finally, I am indebted to the Calouste Gulbenkian Foundation for its support in producing this book.

Peter Wilson
Director of YoungMinds and child psychotherapist

"The emotional development of children must continue to be a central concern for mainstream education."

Department for Education and Department of Health (1994). *The Education of Children with Emotional and Behavioural Difficulties*. Page 10. DFE 9/94: DH LAC (94) 9. London: Department for Education.

"In terms of human survival, managing our emotions and social relationships is perhaps the single most important challenge that faces the human race."

Weare, K. (2000). *Promoting Mental, Emotional and Social Health – a whole school approach*. London: Routledge.

"The one thing I've learned last year is that it's very hard to teach or inspire anyone to do anything unless they've got their personal lives sorted out."

Jamie Oliver in *What happened to Jamie's kids?,* The Guardian, August 27 2003.

Contents

Introduction

This book is about the minds of young people growing in our schools. The development of young minds and the building of our schools are vital for the future of our society – and both are very much our business. All of us have been through school. We all have our memories – our friends, our teachers, our triumphs, our difficulties. Many of us have children and grandchildren in the middle of it all. All of us know about the schools in our neighbourhoods. We pay for them. Everything about schools is a part of us.

We all have experience from our own lives, of how our own minds have developed during our school years and both before and beyond.

How well young minds and schools mix depends on many factors. Children bring into schools their own unique make-ups and their experiences in their families and neighbourhoods. So too do governors, teachers, learning assistants, mentors, and caretakers and all. Schools are made up of the interplay – the dance – of the many relationships of all these people.

At the centre of it all is the primary task of schools to educate – to inform, train, stimulate and prepare the young for adult life.

To achieve this, schools have to carve out their own identities, evolve their own cultures, and bring some kind of coherence to their whole experience. The more they can accomplish this, the more they can build whole school policies on behaviour and bullying and provide all the support that is needed for pastoral care and classroom management. All of this serves to create effective learning environments in which both academic learning and emotional literacy are encouraged.

Schools play such a crucial role in cultivating the intellectual, social and emotional lives of children. They can make such a substantial contribution to the emotional well-being and mental health of their pupils. It is in the very process of education that physical and mental health are enhanced; equally it is out of physical and mental health that the learning potential of pupils is increased.

All young people have their share of stress and problems.

They all face similar pressures and challenges as they grow up and go through school. Most young people meet them with curiosity and enthusiasm and benefit from what school offers. However, some pupils in schools – not an insignificant minority – find it hard to learn and make the most of their abilities. It is important that schools understand the nature of these difficulties and find ways of helping these pupils in the process of improving their learning. It is helpful too if they can come to terms with the different words that are used by different agencies to describe pupils who have very similar problems. In this book, 'mental health problems and disorders' are taken to be very similar to 'emotional and behavioural difficulties'. These problems and difficulties contribute to some, but not all, learning difficulties.

There is a great deal that schools can do to enable young people to become more resilient – and to prevent further disturbance and disruption in their lives. Teachers have a unique role to play in building the strengths and capacities of their pupils. All pupils need to feel accepted and valued in their schools, secure in the knowledge that teachers will not give up on them.

Ultimately in schools, so much depends on the capacity of teachers to go about their work with understanding and support. Not all teachers feel ready or capable of dealing with all the emotional problems in front of them – but all have a responsibility to find ways of enabling their pupils to learn. Teachers need all the support they can get to develop the emotional literacy and the mental health of their pupils.

I hope that this book will give them some of the support they need.

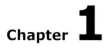

Chapter 1

Our schools

Aren't schools extraordinary places?

There they sit as such an ordinary part of our community and yet what is going on inside them is so full of life and vitality, of energy and variety. However different they may be, they are all simply extraordinary.

Just think about what we expect of them. We place great trust in them to take care of our children. We want them to make our children happy and bright. We'd like them to enrich and cultivate the higher possibilities of their minds. We look to them to make our children fit and healthy and full of character. We demand that they build and prepare our children for the responsibilities of adult life. Increasingly, we require that they make sure they teach our children all the skills and competences that will bring them the high academic results that we all need to feel reassured about – to ultimately secure the good life for our children (and ourselves).

A touch overstated? Possibly, but deep down in most parents' hearts and hopes, in whatever school, in whatever neighbourhood, these kind of expectations are not really far away.

Of course, why not? People want the best for their children

and schools are the places to look to – unquestionably powerful and influential. We all know how important school is for young people. It is a place where they and their friends go to work and play. It is a place where they meet and learn from each other, from friends their own age and from people older than themselves – older children, interesting adults, teachers. It is a place where they can find out about themselves and about the world they are growing up into. It is, above all, a lively and busy place, a community – a place to belong to, beyond the domain of their homes, in the midst of their neighbourhoods, a part of the wider world.

There is in all of this great possibility and much to be done. The potential of a school – through its culture and knowledge, its pastoral provision and classroom management – to create an environment full of learning, is just enormous.

But of course all of this is a tall order. A very tall order. To really meet all these expectations and fulfil the potential, just a few basic things need to be sorted out.

- Buildings need to be secure, safe and well equipped
- Teachers need to be well trained and supported
- Class sizes need to be smaller
- Schools need to be better valued and treasured by the community

Above all, for schools to work at their best, teachers need to be cherished. Excessive bureaucracy and the relentless pressure to reach performance targets do little to improve the enjoyment of teaching. Teaching requires time and reflection. Time – to prepare lessons, to attend to the different needs of children, to mark work and to learn. Reflection – to improve understanding of the learning process, both the academic and the emotional. At its best, teaching should be fun, serious pleasure. Of course it's hard work, but teachers know it's worth it.

The challenges facing schools

However, we cannot deny that most teachers are facing

increasing challenges in the context of the society in which we are all now living. Few can look away from the fact that we are in the midst of some fundamental changes in the ways in which we live – changes which are inevitably having a major bearing on the ways in which children and young people think and behave in our schools.

Here are some of the major social trends that are affecting our everyday lives. During the last 40 years or so, there has been a significant increase in:

- Divorce, lone parents and reconstructed families
- A growing number of children living below the poverty line
- An increasingly socially mobile population
- A growing number of young people, especially young men, without qualifications or prospects of work
- A greater emphasis on testing and exam success at schools
- An increase in the commercialisation of children's activities
- A greater exposure to the influence of the media and wider range of information via the internet
- An increase in the availability of illegal drugs

The impact of all of these changes, accumulating so rapidly in recent years, is difficult to measure. Major demographic changes affecting so many parts of our society and the mounting threat of terrorist acts add to a general sense of unease and uncertainty. We are living in a very different world from the one that existed only a few decades ago and it is our schools that are in the middle of it all. Whatever may happen, schools just have to keep alert to what is new and different and adapt as best they can to greater diversity, different aspirations and assumptions and different ways of doing things from the 'old' (still fairly recent) ways.

It is likely for example that more children come to school these days in a greater state of insecurity than was the case in the past – less sure of their place in their families, more anxious about parental worries and about jobs and money. It is likely too that they come to school with a much wider range of information, of visual impressions and imagery in their minds – tuned in as they are to the amazing technology of our times, the computer and the internet. It is probably less likely that they are prepared to wait their turn, be patient or toler- ant – such is the sense of rush, immediacy and pressure that increasingly grips our culture, not least commercially, to have now and buy now. It is also less likely that they will have the same kind of faith that they may have had in the past in edu- cation for long-term security in work. Indeed it is less likely that they, especially teenagers, come to school fresh-minded and unclouded by the influence of drugs or alcohol from the nights or weeks before.

Of course, it just isn't the case that all teachers are strug- gling all the time with these kinds of pressures, or that the majority of young people can't make the most of the possibil- ities and opportunities of our times. Most teachers and young people will rise to and take new challenges. The question remains, however – how can we make sure that all our schools are equipped and encouraged to meet the new pressures, the new requirements and expectations that they face? How do we ensure that our schools meet the high aspirations that we have of them and take care not only of the academic requirements but also of the social and emotional lives of our pupils as they learn to grow?

Schools must have vision

For a school to be effective, it has to be open to look and take stock of itself. It has to be clear about its objectives and how it plans to reach them. Above all else, a school has got to have a vision of what it is about. This may sound lofty and rather vague. But the key issue here is one of identity, of coherence, of building values that are core to its culture. In a place so full of drive and difference, the key question is simply this: does everything pull together so that everyone knows where they are and where they are going?

It matters that everyone has a hold of this vision and that, in their own different ways, they all sign up to it. This isn't easy. It takes some doing. It takes some time and forbear-

ance, and it includes the involvement of everybody in the school – governors, pupils, teachers, learning assistants, school nurses etc. Any kind of gathering of people in the school is an important event: each is part of a process of finding and developing a sense of purpose without which a school can so easily flounder. Governors' meetings and senior management meetings are crucial to building and sustaining a culture of school life that needs to be inclusive. So too are INSET and away days. School councils are now an integral part of school life cultivating a sense of belonging among pupils and drawing on their views for the improvement of school life. They work by having pupil representatives from each class who have been elected by a peer group. In some schools, these representatives go forward to sit on school governing bodies and even help support new school staff.

Of course people will differ in how they see a school progressing. Some will demand academic achievement, whilst others will have broader educational ambitions. Some may demand greater structure and discipline than others. But what matters is that, whatever the differences, there is a capacity within the school to create a kind of harmony, which is interesting to everybody. Harmony is not simply conformity: it involves dissonance – it's this that makes for a compelling sound. The school is not unlike an orchestra. It needs a conductor to lead – but also many others, playing their parts, keeping to a score, in tune and in rhythm with each other. The more staff and pupils can contribute to the music, the greater the chances are that they will be more involved and motivated to play. Here are just some of the questions that need to be raised at all levels in order to build the vision.

- What do pupils require in order to be creative and productive human beings?
- What do teachers need to develop their skills and build their relationships with each other and with their pupils?
- What does the school need to sustain its momentum and sense of purpose?
- What is everyone going to do about behaviour and about discipline?
- Who is going to write the whole school behaviour and bullying policies and how?
- On what basis and rationale is the school going to exclude pupils?
- What kind of community does the school serve?
- What kind of adults does the school want to develop for the community?
- How best can the school involve parents in the life of the school?
- What is the right balance between ensuring that the academic requirements of the school curriculum are met and attending properly to the emotional and social needs of its pupils?

These questions take everybody to all corners of the school. They need to be gathered and opened for discussion by a leader who has confidence in his or her own ability to hold and contain the anxiety of so much enquiry. Headteachers have a central role to play in promoting this process. They need all the training and guidance they can get to sustain this endeavour. School governors and senior management teams are so important to help fortify this sense of direction that ultimately sets a tone throughout the school.

Creating a healthy school culture

What stands out in all of this is the presence and inspiration of a school culture – a school culture that is healthy. Health is about well-being. It is about functioning effectively, on all cylinders. It is about strength. A school culture needs to be strong enough to create and hold policies that involve the whole school. It's not by chance that the original word for health was 'whole'. Schools with healthy cultures are more likely to create effective learning environments.

Safety and anti-bullying

What matters above all else in these cultures is the importance of ensuring safety for all who work and learn in the school. Establishing fair and consistent discipline is basic. It is, if nothing else, a sign of respect for everybody. Pupils by and large simply cannot apply their minds to their work if they are looking over their shoulder half the time. Pupils need to know where they stand, where they are supposed to be and what to do. They need structure to feel safe, and they need protection from intimidation of any kind – from bullying, racism, sexism or any form of abuse or violence. They need to know that this kind of behaviour is not tolerated by anybody in the school and that when problems do occur, they will be dealt with as speedily and as fairly as possible. It is no longer acceptable for any school, no matter how violent the media or its surrounding neighbourhood may be, to allow violence and intimidating behaviour. An anti-bullying policy is an integral part of a healthy culture.

However, as we all know bullying, as well as being brutal, is insidious and devious – and increasingly invisible through the use of mobiles and text messages. For an anti-bullying policy to really work, the culture of the school has to be such that everyone can be honest, open and involved all the time about what is going on. Bullying needs a constant watchful eye – it won't go away without a clear policy. Teachers, pupils and parents need to have opportunities to talk about it without fear or retribution. The more they are involved in thinking about the problem and working out how best to deal with it, the more they will have an investment in the anti-bullying policy succeeding. The most effective anti-bullying policies have clear guidelines for action and these must be followed through and regularly reviewed.

Building effective schools and emotional literacy

Beyond the fundamental necessity of securing safety, schools that are effective have other major characteristics in common. They all place particular emphasis on raising children's self-esteem. They provide positive feedback. They focus on the importance of achievement in the curriculum and hold high expectations of all children regardless of their particular difficulties.

They also pay particular attention to the social and emo-

tional development of pupils. It is here that schools have such a crucial role to play in enhancing the mental health of pupils – that is to say, in improving their emotional well-being and general resilience. When it comes down to it, mental health refers to the basic human capacity to live a full and productive life. In pupils, it is about the capacity to learn, to meet challenges, to develop talent and ability. All of this is a vital part of growing – it is about building the readiness to take on the challenge of becoming an adult. Some recent studies[1] have found that mentally healthy personality traits in childhood (as measured, for example, on a high score for good peer relations and a low score for anti-social behaviour) are as important predictors of earnings and employment as academic achievement.

Integral to the promotion of pupils' learning and mental health in schools is the development of a culture of emotional literacy and the encouragement of emotional intelligence in children. These are concepts that have gained increasing currency in recent years. They are very important, capturing as they do a wealth of teaching experience over the years and building on increasing research evidence[2]. Essentially, what we are talking about is that everyone in a school should be enabled to understand and manage the variety of emotions that arise in their everyday lives that affect their attitudes and behaviour. It is all about everyone having greater awareness of themselves and others and harnessing their feelings to improve their capacity to learn and to enjoy relationships.

In order to bring all this alive in a school, it is first and foremost important that the whole school, e.g. governors, the headteacher, senior management and the school council embrace the idea of the emotional literacy approach. For emotional literacy to be properly developed in the school, it must be welcomed and respected in all the various ways that it can be carried out. Clearly, it sits very well within the Personal, Social and Health Education (PSHE) curriculum. However, at its best, emotional literacy is taught as part of the very fabric of the school. Fundamental to it all is the attitude and behaviour of as many teachers in the school as possible – that they accept that the more pupils are free to express their feelings and to make sense of them in the context of their everyday life at school, the more likely it is that they will become more attentive, more open to new ideas and more willing to work. Spending time talking and listening to pupils is not a waste – however pressing the demands of the curriculum may be.

There are many other initiatives that can be made to encourage and build emotional literacy in the school.

Peer involvement

Children and young people clearly have a major influence on each other. How they, as peers, live with each other in schools is key to the overall development of emotional literacy in schools. Various initiatives can be made to encourage and develop their potential to help and support each other. Peers can take different roles.

Peer mentoring – guiding other pupils in their studies and helping them to find their place in their schools. They may, for example, offer to help with reading or maths; or provide extra support to those with special needs.

Peer mediation – helping other pupils, in a structured way, to deal more effectively with their quarrels and disputes.

Peer counselling – listening and enabling other pupils to understand their problems better and find their own solutions.

All of these peer initiatives need to be underpinned by training and supervision. It is important that pupils know the limits of what they can do and know who to refer to in the staff when more difficult problems arise.

Nurture groups

These are groups that are set up in schools specifically to understand and meet the emotional needs of those children who have difficulties in learning and relating to others. Some may be disruptive and destructive; others, depressed or withdrawn. These groups provide children with an experience that is nurturing – an experience that they probably missed when they were younger. The groups are small: 10 to 12 children with two or more adults. They are situated within school accommodation and children keep regular contact with their class. Children learn to gain trust and confidence in them; they have the opportunity to build close relationships with adults.

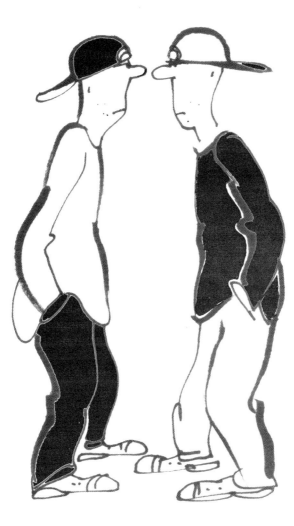

They experience being valued and receiving thoughtful attention in a well-structured, warm and homely atmosphere. The
overriding aim is to integrate these children back into ordinary
classes.

Circle time

This draws on the experience of therapists and practitioners over the years who have understood the value of people getting to know each other in group settings, sharing feelings with each other and learning from each others' experience. Circle time can be a very valuable way of enabling pupils to develop their emotional and social awareness. It provides time to think and reflect and to understand better the events and difficulties that arise in a school day. In some schools, particularly primary schools, circle time is a regular formal part of the day. It is generally facilitated by teachers and guided by ground rules agreed by pupils about how best the group should be run. Circle time can cover a wide range of subjects of relevance to pupils and staff. It has a key role to play in building emotional literacy – helping to cultivate pupils' sensitivities, enabling them to understand how they and other people feel and do things.

Support groups

These are groups which may not necessarily be part of the school routine nor with such a wide agenda as circle time. They may be arranged to meet the particular needs of certain groups of young people at certain times, e.g. those whose parents are going through a family breakdown or divorce, or those with particular difficulties such as Attention Deficit Hyperactivity Disorder (ADHD). In a carefully run group, pupils can gain a great deal of reassurance by realising that they are not the only ones experiencing their particular problems.

Circle of friends

This is a very useful arrangement whereby a group of peers can make themselves available to those pupils who feel isolated and lonely and have difficulty in relating to others. It is a structured intervention that enables pupils to offer friendship and support to others who are more vulnerable and isolated.

In view of the difficulty that teachers have in finding sufficient time to give individual attention to young people in their care, the circle of friends is a very reliable and creative development to draw pupils into offering various kinds of peer support. Peers are an under-used resource and peer initiatives can be a positive way of giving them some responsibility and support. It can be a real benefit for both the recipients and providers.

Making time to listen and talk

Pupils have a lot on their minds other than the subject matters at hand. They may be concerned about circumstances at home – for example, about divorce or domestic violence. They may be upset about a topic which may have been discussed in a lesson. The whole point of emotional literacy is to help pupils to think more about these experiences. It can encourage them to learn more about themselves and thus heighten their interest and motivation to learn in general. There is so much to talk about and so much to put into words. Of course teachers have a great deal of work to do; they have a curriculum, tests to prepare for, examination results to achieve. Of course they don't have the time to talk all day. But they can think imaginatively and practically. They can find ways of making time for pupils to just sit and share their experiences for a while. They can, for example, simply arrange a brief 'talk' time, five minutes or so before a class begins, to help pupils clear their minds of what may have happened previously during the day, in the classroom or playground. This can take out some of the tension and worry of what might have happened. In some schools, a special room may be set aside as a special refuge for those who become very tense or agitated. Sometimes this room is called the 'quiet place'.

Involving parents and carers

So much of the emphasis of this book is on schools being ours. We all have a stake in how our schools are developing. A significant proportion of us are in fact parents and carers and clearly we have a particular interest in what is going on. In order for schools to honour their commitment to their commu-

nities and to learn from the knowledge that parents have of their children, it is important that schools find ways of working collaboratively with people in the community (e.g. local projects, leaders and participants, businesses) and act, as much as possible, with parental involvement. Keeping in touch with and informing parents and carers of their children's progress is basic good practice in schools and contributes significantly to the well-being of all children. Involving parents and carers of children who are having problems is especially important.

The expectations that children have of their teachers (and the lessons) may be influenced quite strongly by their experiences of adults at home. It can help a great deal, therefore, to find ways of meeting and getting to know parents and carers from early on. Most are very concerned about their children, and when difficulties arise, there is much to be gained from listening to them and learning how best to help them. The sooner problems are shared between parents, carers and teachers, the greater the possibility of preventing things getting out of hand, both at home and at school.

It is important to have the parents' and carers' understanding and agreement to a child being referred for professional help outside the school. Every effort needs to be made to help the child cope with juggling school and keeping appointments with the professional concerned. In cases of suspected sexual abuse, it is necessary to follow child protection procedures.

References

1.   For an example of a recent study, see Feinstein, L. (2001). *The relative economic importance of academic, psychological and behavioural attributes developed in childhood.* Presented to Institute for Public Policy Research seminar on Mainstreaming Mental Health in Schools, London, 2 March 2001.

2.   Goleman, D. (1996). *Emotional Intelligence: why it can matter more than IQ.* London: Bloomsbury.

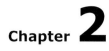

Our young minds

Influences on children from outside schools

Children come to school with a lifetime of experience. This may seem obvious, but schools often forget that there are many strong influences at play during a school day other than those that originate within the school. These are influences that emerge from earlier family life and during the course of a child's maturation and development. It's as well for schools to know something about this and what they are taking on.

Early childhood development

Way before children enter school, their minds have been in continuous formation. From the moment of birth, and indeed before, their minds have been in a progressive state of motion and change. The brain itself has been especially active in the early months and years of life. We now know, from recent advances in brain research[1], that the human brain is not a static organ largely set from the beginning under the exclusive control of the genes. Rather it is a growing, living organism, highly sensitive to and influenced by its surrounding environ-

ment. The capacity for abstract thought and for all of those processes which make up the learning experience – for example planning, directing attention, delaying gratification, regulating states of feeling – is something that is essentially cultivated through experience. These processes all reside in different parts of the brain (largely in the frontal and pre-frontal cortex) and are responsive to the quality of care and stimulation in the child's environment.

We've also learnt a great deal in recent years about the importance of babies and children developing secure attachments in their early experience in their families. A great deal of research[2] has highlighted the fundamental need in young human beings for security – especially at times of threat to their existence. Babies search actively for a parent who will provide warmth, safety, comfort and companionship.

The coming together of these two areas of research – in brain development and early infant attachment relationships – has produced a remarkable amount of evidence, which underlines very clearly the importance of basic human relationships in the process of human growth and learning.

What children need

Put simply, children's brains and minds grow – their emotional and intellectual life develops – in response to their emotional needs being met. Babies need to feel well nourished, securely attached to their mothers and fathers, free from sudden or untoward intrusions. They need to feel contained – that is, deeply understood and held emotionally. Children and young people need to feel loved: they need consistency, continuity and a sense of order in their lives. They need boundaries and limits – to know where they stand with other people and to help them control and channel their energies. These are basic needs that remain largely unchanged as children grow older. Primary school age pupils especially need clear structure in their lives – they look for a sense of certainty and the opportunity to classify and put things into order. They need rules and instructions and above all stimulation and teaching to match their growing cognitive capabilities. They need the security to feel free to play, to experiment and to allow for their curiosity to take them to new discoveries.

Teenagers need much the same, though maybe in a different way. They have much on their minds – not least their own changing bodies and new questions about their identities and futures. They are very much caught up in the intensity of their emotions and in the excitement of their ideas as their minds develop more sophisticated ways of thinking and understanding the world.

But in the midst of all of this, they still basically need the same sense of containment, as they did as children – the same experience of order and boundary in their lives within a secure set of relationships. Teenagers need their privacy – yet always within a context that is clear and committed to them – knowing that they are being thought about and cared for. They need a family and a school that encourages and appreciates their new capacities and gives them room to develop their own personalities and solutions.

What children don't need

It follows from what has been said that what babies and children do not need is any excessive or sustained form of disturbance to their sense of security. No parent or teacher can provide, of course, any kind of perfect state of safety and order but much can be done to prevent abuse: whether it be physical, sexual or emotional. Abuse is essentially intrusive and traumatic – the child is left overwhelmed with experiences that he or she cannot make sense of or adequately process. Without an adequate diet and decent housing, for example, it is less likely that a child will be healthy and strong enough to concentrate at school. Without the experience of secure attachments, it is unlikely that a child will feel sufficiently confident to be ready and open to new opportunities in learning.

We now know much more clearly that young children growing up in conditions of fear and disruption with insecure attachments are less likely to be able to make the most of the opportunities of school life. From brain research[3], we know that, in the brain, under these conditions, a flight/fight response will be stimulated and the right hemisphere become hyper-aroused. This means that children are likely to become hyperactive, restless or impulsive with difficulty in concentrating (especially in boys) or become very withdrawn or cut off (more so in girls). Likewise, from observations of early mother/child attachments, we can see that where children have for various reasons felt insecure in relation to their parents – unsure of the reliability of their parents' love – they are more likely to behave in a restless or unsettled way.

A great deal depends on how parents feel and respond to their children from early on. Some are ambivalent – sometimes they are very loving, other times not so. Children of these parents can't make out what is going on – and they can be very demanding, frantic almost, in a bid to claim their parents' love. Other parents are less emotionally involved with their children, more preoccupied within themselves and often depressed. Children feel they can't make adequate contact: they become quite sad and hopeless – giving up, seeming 'independent', but quite dejected. Some families are so disorganised, lacking in any predictable care or clear boundaries, that children have no idea what is going on or who to depend on. Not surprisingly, their behaviour often becomes erratic and out of control – though some become listless and despairing.

Influences on children from inside schools

Children, then, come into the school and go through school with very different family experiences and in different states of mind. A combination of factors – some inherent within them, others from their experiences in their family and neighbour-hood lives – produce children in different states of readiness to learn. Schools are the recipients of so much that has gone before and that is going to go on besides. This is an important point – to put into some perspective the extent of the school's influence. However healthy a school culture may be and how-ever competent its teachers may be, there is always a limit to what can be achieved with any given child.

However, the excitement of school life resides in its creativ-ity, which is born of the joining and the clashing of different levels of experience – the child's growing mind, with all that is within and behind it, and the sheer force and reality of the school culture. There is so much that is going on in school that can make such a difference to whoever might come into it. It is important to remember that, however crucial early infant mental health experiences are, the brain continues remarkably to be in formation throughout the teenage years until approx-imately the age of eighteen. It matters how teenagers are treated.

Making the most of schools

In the course of school life there are many possibilities and opportunities; and there are many challenges and, for some, troubling experiences. Throughout, most pupils find ways of getting along with other people and working out how best to study and work. They develop the capacity to concentrate, tol-erate frustration and put up with not knowing.

They need to be brave enough to make mistakes, they need

to find a way of linking up different experiences they have gone through, and to take all kinds of decisions about what they say, do and write down. School is busy. How pupils manage everything depends a great deal on their own personal resources, their family circumstances and the social, economic and cultural backgrounds from which they come. The majority do well enough and some do brilliantly. But none are perfect. They are at times moody, unpredictable and fed up. Some go through distressing times at home and have to deal with painful losses of different kinds – they may well be sad, angry and resentful. All of these reactions are natural; they are part and parcel of dealing with the inevitable frustrations and adversities of life.

Resilience and mental health

What matters is that they do not become overwhelmed by their feelings and experiences. The majority of pupils are remarkably resilient – whatever the odds, they are able to learn from their difficulties and make the most of their abilities. They are curious about what is going on and interested in how they feel and make sense of the world. They want to know more about themselves, their friends, their families, their communities and beyond. They are for the most part happy, assertive and confident. They are prepared to try out new experiences and take risks without being destructive to themselves or to others. They have the qualities which most parents would like to see in their children – qualities that make up in effect what we would call the mental health of children. Clearly, families from different cultures and ethnic backgrounds will value certain qualities and principles more highly than others according to their own beliefs and ways of working.

There is so much in these pupils that we can learn from – and make the best use of in our education of all children. We know, for example, that resilient children generally are those that have grown up in their early years enjoying the experience of secure attachments with their mothers as well as their fathers. The majority all seem to have grown up with an easy, outgoing temperament and with authoritative parents who have loved them and set clear and firm boundaries. By and large too they have lived in decent housing with a relatively high standard of living in a wide social and family network. Largely as a result of these positive qualities and circumstances, they have been able to build various capacities that have held them in good stead at school – for example, to plan, to reflect, to communicate readily, to be pro-active and creative in their problem solving.

Mental health and emotional and behavioural problems

Not all children, however, are able to muster the resolve and determination to thrive and enjoy life and school in the same way. Unlike resilient or mentally healthy children, they get stuck, overcome and unable to get on with their lives. They are in various ways less alert and ready to engage with the classroom tasks. Many appear pre-occupied, distracted, and lost in their own thoughts. Some are sad, others angry, others mistrustful. Many just retreat from the life of the classroom – they seem afraid, fearful of mixing with others, cautious about attempting work, distant and unresponsive to the teacher. Others are more restless, unable to settle or concentrate; sometimes they are very dependent and clingy, at other times aggressive and violent. Whether they are inclined to withdraw or to act out – and some children do both, often unpredictably – the ultimate problem they face is their failure to learn. They cannot enjoy the benefits of the school experience. They may be simply too tired, unwell or discontented to care about what school has to offer. They may be out of tune with what is going on, unable to cope with or respond to instructions, take in and digest what is being said. Others may just not turn up to school – either out of fear of the school or out of defiance. There are still others who are so caught up in their battle with authority or with their own personal fears that they seek to destroy the constructive work of others through disruptive, damaging and bullying behaviour. Some may be finally excluded from school – an outcome that can only further deprive them of the crucial experience of belonging and learning that they crave.

The tragedy in all this is that they lack the courage to be

curious or the freedom to discover. In a very real sense they have serious learning difficulties. The causes of such difficulties are numerous. Some again are inherent within the child such as chronic physical illness or developmental disorder in speech and language. Others are more to do with environmental factors, within the family or the neighbourhoods in which they live. A major difficulty resides in their difficulty in forming relationships, in allowing themselves to trust or rely on others, whether friends or teachers. Many may have experienced a great deal of rejection, humiliation or betrayal at home. They may not have benefited from the secure attachments of the resilient child. Many may have experienced a great deal of parental conflict; some of domestic violence. Others may have been subjected to hostility or abuse – physical, sexual, or emotional – or have had to find ways of making sense of inconsistent and sometimes harsh discipline. Some may well have had parents whose own psychiatric illness or alcohol or drug misuse have made it difficult for their parents to provide reliable and consistent care. Yet others may have had to deal with the death of a parent or sibling or friend, with which they have not been able to come to terms.

Many learning and behavioural difficulties are due to the emotional problems that arise as a result of an accumulation of unfavourable circumstances such as these. Most of these children have different kinds of mental health problems or disorders and a small proportion have mental illnesses.

It is important to sort out what we mean by these different terms. People get so confused and mostly think about illness whenever the word 'mental' is used. They then become frightened and think that it has got nothing to do with them. It matters that we don't think of mental health problems as only the business of psychiatrists. These kind of problems are very much part of school experience and are the concern of teachers and all who are involved.

What we really have in mind when we use the word 'mental' is simply – the mind. And we all have minds. We all have mental experiences. If we didn't, we would all be plain boring. Schools are all about building the minds of young people. The fact is that we all go through a wide range of feelings and thoughts in our lives which, at different times, may get on top

of us. They can become unmanageable and lead us to do things that we wouldn't ordinarily do. We may have many problems on our minds that we do not always have the strength or capacity to deal with. Sometimes these problems will pass with the help of family and friends. Sometimes they don't, and they can in various ways seriously interfere with our happiness and everyday lives. When we talk of mental health problems and disorders we are talking about different degrees of difficulty. There is no one simple divide between mental health and mental illness. We all sit at different times and in different ways along what can be best called a continuum of mental health.

The term 'mental health problems' refers more or less to the same difficulties that children have as does the term 'emotional and behavioural problems'. Children with these kinds of problems show different kinds of behaviour in the classroom – they may be attention seeking, fidgety, aggressive, unable to concentrate; or withdrawing, unresponsive, with few friends, physically unwell or tired. Some of these problems may be manageable in the classroom, with extra support, within a healthy school culture. However, others are more serious. They don't pass – and they can so easily build up to cause a great deal of disturbance to the children themselves and those who care for and teach them.

Few can be said to enjoy complete mental health – yet few are so disturbed as to be diagnosed as having a mental illness such as schizophrenia, clinical depression or extreme anorexia nervosa. By and large they are not so confused that they cannot distinguish between reality and fantasy. But nevertheless they are often very distressed and overwhelmed and have difficulty in dealing with the strains and pressures of everyday life and the demands of growing up. These children in other words have a wide range of mental health problems – some very apparent at school, others more covered up and more of a problem at home. Child and adolescent mental health specialists often refer to children with the more severe, the more persistent problems, as having mental disorders.

Mental disorders

The term 'mental disorder' is a term that refers to serious and complex mental health problems that persist over time and cause a great deal of disturbance to children and their families. These disorders matter because they interfere significantly with the children's everyday lives and development.

Mental disorders come in many forms and focus largely on the behaviour (or conduct) of the young person and on their emotional states such as phobias, obsessions and eating preoccupations. For a full discussion of these disorders read the *Mental Health Handbook for Schools* by Mary Atkinson and Gary Hornby.

- *ADHD*

Some children and young people suffer from an inability to focus their attention and control their impulsive behaviour. In the majority of cases, both biological and environmental factors play a part in bringing about the disorder. It is important that parents, teachers and specialist mental health practitioners work in collaboration in assessing and developing ways of managing the behaviour.

- *Behavioural problems*

These are problems that arise from the aggressive, impulsive or unusual ways that some children behave. They cause distress and disruption to the children and young people themselves and to those who care for them at home or at school.

- *Conduct disorder*

This is a term that covers a wide range of behaviour, which is generally aggressive and anti-social. This behaviour (conduct) repetitively and persistently interferes with the lives of other people as well as the child's own emotional, social and intellectual development. It includes bullying, initiating fighting, stealing, destroying property, running away and truanting. It is the most commonly referred mental health disorder and, if left untreated, it can persist into major behavioural and personality problems during adolescence and in adult life. Over 90% of juvenile offenders who repeatedly commit crime have had a conduct disorder as a child.

- *Depression*

Many children and young people feel depressed from time to time in response to disappointments and losses of different kinds in their lives. Clinical depression or depressive illness are terms used to refer to extreme feelings of depression that persist over time, seemingly often unrelated to any particular current experience. The most common symptoms are low mood, feelings of worthlessness, loss of appetite, inability to sleep, social withdrawal and loss of interest in study, work or relationships.

- *Eating disorders*

These are problems that many children, and especially

teenagers, have in taking in and digesting food and drink. Some young people persistently refuse to eat to the point where their physical growth and health are seriously damaged. These young people suffer from anorexia nervosa. Others binge and then vomit with similar damage to their health; these suffer from bulimia nervosa.

• *Emotional disorders*

All children and young people experience a wide range of feelings and emotions during the course of their development. Anger, fear, jealousy, rivalry, love, hatred are but a few. It is through experiencing these emotions that children learn about themselves and their relationships. Emotional experiences can be both joyful and painful; this is all part of normal growing up. It is when children become overwhelmed by the intensity and the persistence of the feelings that disturb them, that they begin to experience problems and disorders. This interferes with their ability to enjoy life and function well at home and at school. Some emotional problems can become particularly severe and interfere significantly with everyday life. Typical emotional problems and disorders can include fears and pho-bias (of school, of spiders, being trapped in confined places, etc), panic reactions, anxiety about separating from parents and obsessive-compulsive behaviour.

• *Obsessive-compulsive disorder*

This arises from a severe state of anxiety that leads children and young people to become overly preoccupied in repetitive behaviour and rituals, e.g. repetitive hand washing. They become overwhelmed by ideas and feelings that get stuck in their minds – ideas that they do not want, but which persist and cause a great deal of distress and confusion. They inter-fere with children getting on with their everyday life at school and in the community.

• *Psychosomatic disorder*

This is a disorder that has both physical and mental sides to it. The relationship of the body and the mind is a very close and complicated one. It is often difficult to know how far phys-ical symptoms are brought about by mental stress or how far physical problems can lead to mental distress. There is a wide range of symptoms such as headaches, stomach aches, tiredness – symptoms that may be caused or aggravated by mental and emotional factors.

• *Schizophrenia*

Some people may become very confused in their thinking – being illogical and incoherent, not making sense. They may develop beliefs that seem odd and not based on anything that is happening in reality. Some become very suspicious and paranoid and believe that other people are against them or ganging up on them. Others believe that they can see things in people or hear voices or sounds that in reality do not exist. Largely because of these false beliefs (delusions) and perceptions (hallucinations), their behaviour is often strange, bizarre and inappropriate.

Teachers as observers

Schools vary a great deal in their intake but, in most schools, especially those in inner city areas, it is likely that teachers are having to deal with many pupils who are presenting a wide range of difficulties – some academic but many more to do with emotional and behavioural or mental health problems. Teachers are not qualified to diagnose mental disorders. However, they are in a key position to notice signs of such difficulty and distress and to make referrals where necessary. These difficulties may be quite obvious, but in many cases it may take some time for teachers to make sure whether or not they should take further action. Making judgements about the emotional well-being of young people is rarely straightforward and teachers need the chance to check their observations with other staff. It is important to bear in mind that it is very difficult to define one clear 'normal' developmental pathway through childhood and adolescence. Care always needs to be taken to understand and respect the different values of children and families from different backgrounds.

All children of course become preoccupied and worried from time to time with problems at home or at school. They may be

moody and irritable. Their eating and sleeping may be affected, and they may not always have their minds on their work.
There are no children who behave correctly and properly all
the time. Inevitably they make mistakes and get into difficulties. Teenagers in particular can be remarkably unpredictable
and at times rebellious, some becoming quite isolated within
themselves whilst others become more aggressive and intrusive.

All of this is part of growing up, and it is important to keep
some perspective of what can reasonably be called 'normal

development'. It is sometimes best to leave well enough alone, allowing the child the time and opportunity to find his or her own way forward. However, teachers do need to be alert to when problems persist, or interfere significantly with development and learning. The earlier children's difficulties can be identified and dealt with, the greater the chance of preventing larger problems later on.

Some children express themselves well enough through talking; others may prefer writing or artwork. Many children, however, most effectively show what is on their minds through their behaviour and attitude and in the way they relate to each other and to the teachers.

Major signs of pupils in difficulty

- Sudden changes in behaviour, mood or appearance
- Standard of work dropping dramatically
- Becoming subdued or over-excited
- Failing to hand in homework
- Refusing to go to school
- Dressing in a noticeably different style; looking untidy or becoming excessively concerned with cleanliness

General behaviour

- Hyperactive, attention seeking, anxious or restless
- Aggressive, defiant and disruptive of others' work
- Unusually quiet and passive; not in touch with what is going on; withdrawn
- Odd or regressive behaviour; behaving younger than real age
- Appearing tense or unhappy; showing hostility
- Obsessive (e.g. overly tidy, so that little work is done)
- Extremely conscientious, perfectionist, 'too good' (e.g. destroying their work because it is not good enough)

Pattern of work

- Having difficulty settling into any piece of work and concentrating in class

- Losing enthusiasm and motivation
- Becoming overly absorbed in study

Pattern of attendance

- Reluctance to leave school or class
- Arriving early or late every morning
- Missing school or lessons, playing truant
- Refusing to go to school

Relationships

- Having difficulty getting on with other children in the class; having few or no friends

Younger children in particular

- Extremely clingy or demanding of a teacher; frequently breaking down in tears
- Constantly getting into fights with other children and having temper tantrums
- Damaging other children's work
- Insisting on initiating sexual play
- Being very bossy and over-organising others

Older children in particular

- Looking unhappy and solitary, tired or unwell
- Becoming careless or indifferent about work
- Problems with eating (e.g. throwing away packed lunches; losing or gaining weight)
- Being drawn into promiscuity, delinquency or misusing alcohol or drugs
- Violent behaviour in playground or class
- Breaking the law outside school
- Self-destructive behaviour (e.g. arm cutting)

These signs do not automatically mean that a child has an emotional or behavioural difficulty or a mental health problem or disorder, although they may be indicative of one.

Key questions for teachers to keep in mind

- What sort of problem does the child have?
- How best to describe the problem – behaviour, mood, attitude?
- How extreme is the behaviour or attitude?
- How prolonged or persistent is it?
- What has happened in the child's life to initiate this behaviour and attitude?
- Are there sudden changes in behaviour?
- When does the behaviour occur?
- How 'driven' or out of control is the child?
- Is there a marked contrast between the way a child behaves at home and at school?
- How is the behaviour affecting other members of the school community?
- What are the strengths of the child?
- What support and advice is available?

When teachers are having particular difficulties with pupils it may be helpful for them to look critically at what they themselves are doing and what is happening in the school generally. However, it is important that teachers do not see it as necessarily their failure if they cannot handle troubled pupils on their own. It is always important to talk over problems with other staff. Getting outside help for pupils may often be the most positive way of tackling a difficulty before it becomes a crisis. Many problems can be managed on a day-to-day basis at school but there are some which cannot be dealt with in the classroom alone and teachers should not be expected to act as a therapist or social worker.

Arrangements to assist teachers

Different schools have different arrangements to assist teachers. The principal point of reference in most schools is a Special Educational Needs Co-ordinator (SENCO) or Head of Year. Some schools also provide consultation for staff for managing difficult children. The Special Educational Needs Code of

Practice sets out various stages of procedure in which arrangements are made for teachers to keep records of their observations of pupils that they are concerned about and for liaison with other colleagues both in and outside the school. A statement of special needs may be the most effective way of getting support and a multi-agency approach. It can provide a forum for discussion of pupils' needs, exploring the most appropriate support and offering long-term help, which can be systematically reviewed. Monthly staff meetings can address problems relating to particular pupils to make sure that there are consistent approaches to the way they are dealt with in the school. Parents and carers, teachers, child and adolescent mental health specialists, social workers, behaviour support workers, educational psychologists, school nurses, educational welfare officers, Connexions workers, pastoral staff, school counsellors, personal tutors, mentors and GPs can all contribute in different ways. It is not always necessary for particular pupils to be seen by professionals outside the school: it may be sufficient for teachers to talk about the problem with the professionals. This can be a useful process of assessment and can lead to new strategies for support.

Teachers need to keep an accurate and dated record of their observations and concerns so that they can discuss actual events or changes of behaviour with parents and other professionals as and when necessary. It is also essential to know whether pupils have been offered help or are receiving professional help outside the school. It is important to know, for example, whether pupils are on medication for any reason because that may be having an effect on their behaviour. Staff should of course liaise closely with other services, especially on these more serious matters. Teachers sometimes know more than others about pupils' problems and can provide important insights.

What kind of journey through school?

Life is challenging to pupils at all stages of development as they go through school. Times of transition, tackling new subjects, joining new groups, having new teachers, preparing for public examinations – all are critical points in pupils' lives. They open up new possibilities of learning, but equally they present difficulties and pressures, which, for some, can be very difficult to handle.

School transfer can be a time of great stress, particularly for children who have experienced loss or who find coping with change difficult. Most of us experience anxiety at times of change and our ability to cope with it depends on life experiences and the support systems we have in place. Pupils need to be prepared for these changes and be provided with support.

Entry into primary school

The most dramatic change of all is the first move from everyday family life at home to daily life at school. Most children are excited by this experience and are ready to enter into new relationships and make the most of the opportunities that are available. Others, however, are more timid, afraid of losing the familiar protection or proximity of their parents, and overawed by all the new children and adults and the boisterousness of the playground. They may become frightened of going to school, and their parents may find it difficult letting them go. Others may not be able to concentrate and learn or they may deal with their anxieties by becoming disruptive and aggressive. Play group and nursery school can help with this crucial first transition, providing young children with the chance of getting to know other children and adults outside the family, introducing new activities and developing language and social skills.

It is especially important to notice signs of difficulty at this stage and to remember that children are not all the same and will mature and develop at a different rate.

The years that young people spend at primary school are of crucial importance for their intellectual, social and emotional growth, and the development of their self-esteem. Primary school offers pupils the opportunity to establish their own independence from home and to discover all sorts of things about themselves and the outside world beyond their family. They learn about making relationships, and they develop new ways

of thinking. Pupils need a reliable and consistent structure to their day in which to feel secure and learn most effectively. Provided they are well prepared, most are able to respond positively to new experiences. They are curious and ready to develop their capacity to learn. They are interested in exploring their differences and are stimulated by the new competitive challenges. Sudden changes of routine, however, or unexpected activities, can be unsettling for some, at least in the beginning. Teachers and other staff can make a great difference to these young people by allowing them time to adjust and by explaining clearly what is being planned. Teachers need to remember that young people vary a great deal in their maturity and that those who have experienced difficulties in their early childhood may take longer to settle.

The transfer from primary school to secondary school

The move from primary to secondary school is a major event in a young person's life. It represents one of the most significant steps in growing up and achieving greater maturity. Like the earlier move into primary school, it entails the loss of all that has been familiar: teachers, routines, sometimes friends. It is a transition to a different, much larger, more anonymous environment with more people, more strangers and new rules and procedures. The more complex organisation of the secondary school requires pupils to move from one class to another and from one group to another. Pupils can no longer rely on having the same physical place to belong in, or the same students in the form with them. They must also adapt to working with different teachers and more tests and exams.

Again, most pupils react positively to the new regime, but some may feel quite overwhelmed. Some can become very anxious and refuse to go to school at this point in their school lives. Teachers need to be attentive to signs of stress, both in the last term of primary school when children are anticipating the move and in the first year of secondary school after the transition has taken place.

Secondary school life can be a very testing time for young people. They may have difficulty in balancing and dealing with the demands of the curriculum, the pressures of the peer group and their adolescent tasks of growing up.

Teenagers have their own particular problems. They are learning to question authority, challenge assumptions and test limits. They have much on their minds just in growing up – and it's not surprising that they have difficulty in concentrating on their work at times. Most can handle these tensions well enough so they can enjoy their new experiences and still get on with their work. Others however may become too frightened by these changes; they may lose themselves in the excitement of it all or become rigid and controlling. Either way, mental health problems can develop, and teachers need to be aware and monitor and intervene at an early stage.

Good communication between teachers in primary schools and secondary schools can assist pupils through this transition. It is useful for primary schools to help pupils to make a record of everything that they have achieved whilst at primary school.

This can help them to recognise their accomplishments at a time when they may be feeling apprehensive. Programmes can be carried out to let pupils know what secondary school is like so they can learn about new procedures, familiarise themselves with the new subjects on offer and thus feel more prepared. It is particularly important to provide support for those who feel overly anxious. They may need extra visits and they may well benefit from a staff or pupil mentor whom they can get to know prior to the transfer. Pupils from secondary schools can go into feeder primary schools and brief the Year 6 students about the sort of changes to expect and answer their questions. Secondary schools can organise small groups for those experiencing particular difficulty. It matters a great deal to pay attention to any difficulties that may occur at this crucial time; it can certainly prevent a whole range of problems developing later in school life.

Leaving school and examinations

A mounting worry for most young people in the later years of secondary school arises from the question whether or not, and in what ways, they are going to achieve and what they are going to do once they have left school. Many feel under considerable pressure to succeed at school and to pass exams, and some have to struggle to meet high parental or school expectations. The fear of failure can be troubling and for some quite intolerable. They may push themselves too hard and worry excessively, or they may give up and pull out altogether. Some may feel school to be irrelevant to their real lives in the outside world, or for example, (in some areas especially) to the problems of unemployment.

Teachers are in a good position to keep an eye on such strains and to offer help or reassurance, and put things into context. They can tune in to the anxieties young people have about their future and offer as much information and advice as possible to help them prepare. They can also help many pupils who feel too despondent and disaffected to take a more positive attitude to the challenges ahead. However, in the busy timetables of the secondary school, it can be hard to spot problems, and difficult to keep track of those who are in difficulty. How do you look out for a student in one of several teaching groups, when you only see him or her twice a week? Well established pastoral care and tutorial systems are essential to ensure adequate procedures for keeping an eye on pupils who give concern, and for ensuring that problems are not overlooked.

References
1. Murray, L. & Andrews, L. (2000). *The Social Baby: understanding babies' communication from birth.* Richmond, Surrey: CP Publishing. See also Winkley, L. (1999). Neural Pathways and the Development of the Brain. *Primary Practice* No. 20, pp.30-35.
2. Sroufe, L.A. (1998). *Emotional Development.* Cambridge: Cambridge University Press. Also see Crittenden, P.M. & Clausen, A.H. (eds.) (2000). *The Organisation of Attachment Relationships: Maturation, Culture and Context.* Cambridge: Cambridge University Press.
3. Winkley, L. (1999). Neural Pathways and the Development of the Brain. *Primary Practice* No. 20, pp.30-35.

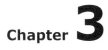

And what of the teachers?

Teachers are crucial

It is difficult to emphasise strongly enough the crucial role that teachers play in educating the minds of young people. By teachers we mean all those who make a significant contribution to helping children learn. They are the people who have such a large part to play in putting into effect the healthy culture of the school. They are the people who help to implement the whole school policies on how the school should be run. They are the people who are there to set an example and to attend as best they can to the social and emotional development of their pupils to facilitate learning. They are the people too to introduce the new methods and the technology to enable pupils to acquire knowledge. Teachers have much to do in attending to the sheer technicality of their work, e.g. reading, preparing and marking work, preparing for standardised tests.

Their task is formidable and none the easier in the face of so much diversity of experience in front of them. Their classrooms are filled with pupils of different abilities and talents; of different levels of intellectual and academic achievement; of different cultural and family backgrounds. Much of the skill of teaching is having the ability to observe and to assess these differences – to determine the pace of academic learning of different pupils and to recognise those who are having difficulties along the way.

Classroom management

Many children's needs can be met within the general management of the classroom setting for all pupils. A great deal depends, for example, on how well teachers can establish a sense of order and safety in the classroom. Classroom activities need to be well prepared and well structured – as far as possible, teachers need to be ahead of the game in terms of how they plan the balance between providing input and having time for activity, participation and discussion. Much depends on timing and pace – and setting expectations of pupils which aren't too high as to be unachievable or too low as to be condescending. It matters that teachers are clear and direct in how they communicate what they are planning and what they expect children to do, with whom and for how long. Routine and predictability, keeping good time and doing what is promised are so basic that it's all too easy to forget how crucial they are. Pupils respond well to being set specific tasks and given clear responsibilities, and to being acknowledged and praised for what they have achieved. It is important that teachers create an atmosphere in the classroom that promotes rather than discourages feelings of competence. There are many tangible ways of logging success whether it be academic or social: with photographs, journals, wall displays, message books, badges, leaflets for parents, special privileges and so on.

Where classroom management is strong and teachers are able to maintain a positive attitude to the demands of so many challenges, it is not only the education of the pupils which is being taken care of but also the mental health problems of those young people who may be in difficulty. Teachers in their primary educational role can provide the right conditions for everyone, especially the more vulnerable and confused, to feel safe and acknowledged.

Pupils with problems

There are some pupils, however, whose problems are clearly beyond the reach of teachers alone. They may be depressed, self-harming and even at times suicidal. In large measure their problems arise from circumstances outside the school, although in some cases they may be made worse by what is happening in school, e.g. bullying. Teachers have a responsibility to be aware of these difficulties and to offer some degree

of help. They are in a pivotal position to serve as a port of call for many pupils who basically are in need of a listening ear. So many pupils may lack the opportunity to share their views with anyone else, even with their parents, relatives or friends. Pupils may have all kinds of difficulties at home – their parents may be separating or divorcing, there may be a death in the family or loss of a friend, they may be enduring hurtful bullying experiences, or worrying about physical and sexual problems. Many of these preoccupations may come to the surface as a result of what has been said or aroused in the normal course of classroom work especially in subjects such as English, PSHE or Physical Education.

The question is – how interested are teachers in the emotional problems of their pupils in class? How interested should they be? Are they sympathetic, thoughtful, ready to help; or impatient, dismissive, "not my concern, I've got a curriculum job to do"? The teacher's general approach is so important, not only in terms of how it may communicate itself to the pupils themselves, but also to the rest of the class – and indeed the whole school. Does this school recognise the emotional life of its pupils and its relation to learning? Is it going to help them find the language to put into words the kind of feelings and thoughts they have in their minds? Is it going to help them manage their difficulties? These are reasonable questions, which have everything to do with the value that many schools, as well as their teachers, place on the role of developing emotional literacy and intelligence in the life of the school.

Teachers who listen

One of the most valuable contributions that teachers can make to the learning of all children, and the more so to those with mental health problems and difficulties in learning, is to listen. Children, in the right frame of mind, often have a great deal to say about themselves – however withdrawn, uncommunicative or indifferent they may seem. Young children in primary school are remarkably expressive in their artwork, making very clear drawings of their experiences of life. Teachers need to be able to understand the meaning of these pictures and find ways of

'talking' to children about their problems through their pictures. Children who feel depressed, for example, often have a
lot to communicate about their sense of hopelessness and
rejection in the face of overwhelming situations at home. They
may feel furious, guilty or sad, for example, about the loss of
a parent (due to death or separation) or a friend (who may
have changed loyalties or moved) or a pet who may have dis-
appeared. Children who are self-harming or are attempting
suicide or having eating problems often have similar feelings
which they express in their different ways; all have much in
common, all attacking their own bodies in one way or another
and secretly.

Listening is very important. It matters simply because it
helps pupils to learn; they feel respected and heard. But, however simple it all may sound, it isn't so straightforward for the
teacher to do all this in the midst of so many pressures and
distractions that make up the life of a busy school day.

Listening takes time and patience. It takes courage too, to
be open to the distress and anguish of so many children's disturbing stories. It isn't easy to listen well, with understanding.
Teachers need support and training to listen properly. It helps,
for example, that they have a framework of understanding to
enable them to make sense of what they are hearing – an
understanding of child development, of family dynamics, of
learning difficulties and emotional and behavioural difficulties
and mental health problems. They need as well good management to allow them to spend more time to listen – to autho-
rise them to spend their time in this way.

It is very important that teachers learn to set their own
boundaries around the process of listening. They have to keep
in mind the whole class, and they have to be careful to protect
individual children from developing too much unrealistic
dependence on them. They need to make it clear to pupils the
limits of what they can do and can't do. Teachers should make
it known to pupils when they are available to talk and how
much time they will have. It is often sufficient just to listen to
the pupils, to convey sympathy and concern and to reflect back
or summarise what is on the pupils' minds. It may be useful
and necessary to follow up with one or two further meetings but
it is generally inadvisable to go beyond this on an individual

basis. Teachers should try to find ways of encouraging pupils to share their problems with other people too – if possible with members of their family. This may be problematic in some cases and it is important that teachers know the full range of support staff in the school to refer to. Confidentiality is clearly a major issue, which needs to be clarified in school policies. Total confidentiality cannot be promised if there is disclosure of possible sexual abuse or ongoing criminal activities, or if there are concerns about contraception and pregnancies. Most pupils understand these boundaries and within them they appreciate being heard and having their problems taken seriously.

Challenging behaviour and ADHD

Some pupils are challenging to teachers. Their behaviour is difficult, defiant, aggressive, seemingly senseless. Their number varies in different schools – but even if only a few, they can be very disruptive to the whole class. Most teachers have had some experience of them and usually feel, in different ways, threatened, undermined and exasperated. At times they may find it necessary to remove these pupils from class – but wherever possible, it is important to work towards keeping them within the normal course of school life. Removal or expulsion only makes worse their underlying insecurity, sense of rejection and anger – and this in turn invariably leads to ever more destructive behaviour. At best, most of these pupils can be contained through fair and consistent discipline in well-structured classes in which they know what is expected from them. They can be contained too through being listened to. It helps if teachers are prepared to stand back and try to look through the difficult behaviour and make sense of its meaning – i.e. what is the pupils' behaviour 'saying'? Pupils who are defiant and careless about their work, for example, may be saying in so many words: "Nobody cares about me. People have been offensive to me in my life. So why should I care and treat them or you with respect? Maybe you will say you respect me, but I'm not going to believe anything until I see proof that you care about me. That's to say, whatever you do, I'll test you. Otherwise why should I care about you or anything?"

Some of these challenging pupils are hyperactive; they are restless, inattentive, and impulsive. They cannot concentrate and they find it difficult to settle or complete assigned tasks. With patience and clear structure in the classroom, however, most are able to keep within the boundaries and gradually learn to manage their behaviour and apply themselves to what is required. Some, however, are not so responsive. Their hyperactive behaviour is persistent; it takes over all aspects of their lives at school and at home, and invariably leads to angry, difficult and anti-social behaviour. It is vital to check on all the various factors that may be exerting an influence on the pupil and to make sure that school is not aggravating the problem.

If all avenues have been explored, then these children need to be referred for specialist help through the SENCO to the local child and adolescent mental health service or paediatric service, and seen for assessment by a child psychiatrist or paediatrician.

Many of these children may well be diagnosed as having ADHD. This basically means that they suffer from deficits in their ability to focus their attention and to control their impulsive behaviour. There seems to be no single cause for such a disorder. In the majority of cases, both biological and environmental factors play a part and it is very important that teachers and child mental health professionals work collaboratively in assessing and developing ways of managing these young people.

For some young people, child psychiatrists or paediatricians may suggest medication to enable them to settle and concentrate enough to benefit from teaching and to take their place appropriately in the classroom without incurring the criticism and hostility which they often arouse. The most common medication is Ritalin. It is important to stress, however, that medication does not cure the condition, nor does it provide a lasting treatment. Moreover, it should not be recommended as the first or only treatment. It should be reserved for certain pupils who have been carefully diagnosed, and seen as part of an overall management approach in which help is given to the family and to the young person both in the child and adolescent mental health service and in the school. It is essential that when a young person is taking Ritalin, the situation is carefully monitored and regularly reviewed.

In the classroom, hyperactive young people and those suffering from ADHD can be helped significantly if time and sufficient attention is given to their needs. It can make a great deal of difference, for example, if they are provided with a clear structured routine in which they are protected from distractions and intrusions. It can help to seat them near the front of the classroom with quieter children – not as a punishment but as a way of helping them calm down. It is important too, to give them clear, simple instructions and allow them extra time to complete their task. Giving them work in smaller units can help to compensate for their short attention span. Teachers need to make frequent contact with them and help build their organisational and social skills. Help with establishing friend- ships through a buddy or mentoring system can be very ben- eficial, so too can offering them special responsibilities so that other pupils see them in a positive light. Children with ADHD often possess artistic and creative talents which can be devel- oped and their achievements need to be recognised. It is essential that teachers be given support, particularly in rela- tion to those pupils who have a persistent difficulty.

Teachers' aspirations

Just as the whole school faces a tall order in meeting the expectations of its parents and communities, so do teachers in juggling so many demands in meeting both the academic and the emotional needs of their pupils. In order to rise to the requirements of the job, teachers need to recognise that at the centre of their work is the importance of their relationship with their pupils. Here is a list[1] of activities that teachers might aspire to – however difficult they may be to carry out at any given moment of any given day.

- Try and see each pupil in a positive light
- Listen to pupils and make time for them individually
- Accept pupils non-judgementally
- Make pupils feel respected and valued
- Provide lots of opportunity for success. Build on pupils' strengths, taking care to grade the steps of teaching to make achievement possible
- Reassure pupils about making mistakes; that this is a part of learning and not a sign of failure
- Provide lots of specific praise and lots of opportunities for celebrating achievement
- Empathise with the pupils' position
- Encourage pupils to take responsibility for themselves and give them a voice and some control
- Treat pupils fairly
- Adopt a participative rather than a confrontational approach

- Always believe in the pupils' ability to learn and to change
- Be prepared to acknowledge teacher fallibility
- Be prepared to analyse practice and change
- Model the behaviours expected from the pupils
- Model emotional literacy
- Nurture teacher well-being
- Recognise that teachers are vital in becoming part of the solution to the stresses that pupils experience

This is a formidable list. It is laudable, necessary, but probably not always possible! Confronted as many teachers are by increasing workloads, mounting bureaucracy, essays to mark and over-sized classes – not to mention the overall strain of meeting performance targets and achieving good test results – it is not surprising that many do not always feel ready or able to meet all these aspirations. Many may feel competent enough to deal with the academic requirements of their subjects but not to take on the emotional and mental health problems of their pupils. It is not uncommon for teachers at the end of the day and especially at the end of the term to feel very drained and exhausted by the sheer weight of their workload.

The interplay between teachers and pupils

To understand something more of the complexity of teachers' tasks and to make greater sense of the difficulties that they encounter, it is useful to focus on the nature of the relationship between pupils and teachers and to think of it as a kind of interplay, a dance in effect. Not in any way a specific tango or hip-hop or pirouette – but rather a kind of interplay in which pupils bring from their past ways of thinking and doing things into the classroom – and the teachers have to find ways of getting the hang of them, fitting in and dancing along with them as best they can. Equally, the other way round, teachers bring in from their pasts their own way of doing things and pupils have to fit in and respond as best they can. And, of course, the more complicated the routine, the more new steps both have to find to dance with each other as creatively as possible – one

leading the way sometimes, the other taking the lead at other times.

The point is that in the classroom, a whole range of interactions build up, in large part determined by what teachers and pupils introduce from their own past and current personal experiences. In the most positive terms, for example, those pupils who feel well in themselves, who have experienced security in their early lives and who possess many of the qualities that make up resilience, come to school with a readiness to be involved and to learn. They are responsive to teachers. The teachers are delighted; they feel appreciated. So in turn do the pupils. The interplay is lively, full of learning. The dance proceeds.

This, of course may sound too wonderful to be true – but, in some schools, where there is a healthy culture and strong classroom management and where the majority of pupils are not overly laden with distressing personal experiences, school life can be fun – at its best, serious fun. However, as we all know, conditions like these do not always prevail in schools, families and communities. The reality is that, in varying degrees, conditions are often difficult, complicated, lacking sufficient resources – and that both pupils and teachers bring into the life of the school many of their own frustrations and conflicts from their lives elsewhere.

Then, too, there is adolescence! Teenagers have their own particular developmental turmoil and confusion – struggling as they are with their changing bodies, with their increasing independence from their parents and with their emerging identity and sexuality. With all of this going on, the dance too often gets out of step, out of rhythm. It can, of course, collapse.

There are many factors that influence the general interplay between teachers and pupils. All kinds of pressures arise from our society as a whole, from the neighbourhoods in which our schools exist, from families, from industry, from government, from academia – all impinge on how people relate to each other in different ways in school. However, in the midst of all of this is this central importance of the nature and capacity for relationship that resides within teachers and pupils – the assumptions, expectations and ways of relating that teachers and pupils bring into the school with them.

There are many ways of understanding these relationships – but some of the most useful insights come from experience and research into what we know from early attachment experiences in childhood. Through this understanding, it is possible to see more clearly some of the patterns of relationships that are laid down in early life – and that then continue into later life and in school. To illustrate this, let's make use of two scenarios.

Two scenarios: from home to school

The first is called *Unhappy interplay at home*. It describes how the dance, the interplay between a mother and her child in the early years can be disrupted and complicated. The second scenario, called *Unhappy interplay at school*, describes the continuation of this dance into the school situation in the relationship between pupil and teacher. Both may seem extreme but are not atypical. They are necessarily simplified to highlight the underlying psychodynamics that can lead to disturbed or challenging behaviour and seriously interfere with the learning process in school.

It is important to emphasise that the feelings described in these scenarios are taken to be basically generated by the nature of the early mother-child relationship of the pupils. These feelings are then seen to be relived in the classroom in relation to the teacher, who in turn has to find ways of dealing with their impact.

Teachers and pupils may not be fully aware of these feelings. For the most part, feelings tend to get expressed in the way both behave. They are not 'bad' or 'wrong' feelings – they simply belong to the relationships that develop. What matters above all else is that the teachers have the opportunity to know and understand them better – not to be caught out by them.

With this self-awareness, they are more likely to be in a better frame of mind to cope more effectively with the difficulties they face. With this knowledge – that the way they feel may well be in response to the strong feelings evoked in them by their pupils – they are less likely to take things too personally, e.g. that they are angry or incompetent failures. With all this in mind, they are less likely to react defensively, e.g. by being rejecting or punitive.

First scenario

The diagram facing[2], *Unhappy interplay at home,* illustrates a difficult attachment between mother and child:

And what of the teachers?

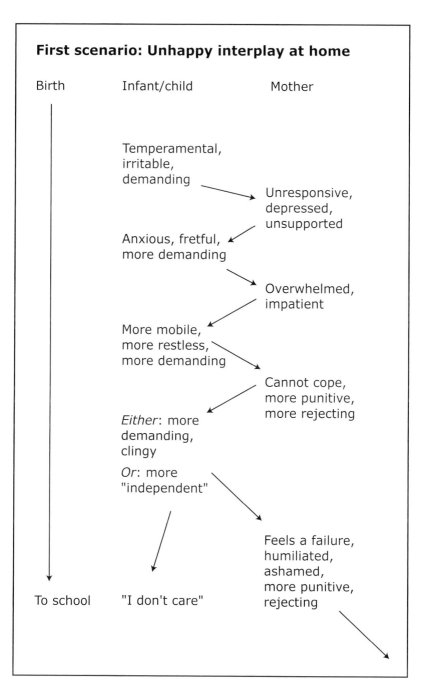

First scenario: Unhappy interplay at home

Birth   Infant/child   Mother

Temperamental, irritable, demanding

Unresponsive, depressed, unsupported

Anxious, fretful, more demanding

Overwhelmed, impatient

More mobile, more restless, more demanding

Cannot cope, more punitive, more rejecting

Either: more demanding, clingy

Or: more "independent"

Feels a failure, humiliated, ashamed, more punitive, rejecting

To school   "I don't care"

In the first scenario, we imagine a sensitive, irritable, temperamental boy being born to a young mother who for various reasons is not ready for her child. She may be depressed, as many mothers are after a birth. Or worse, she may have postnatal depression, which is very serious for both baby and mother. The mother feels unable to care or extend herself to the baby as much as she or the baby would like. The mother may be living in poor housing conditions, with poor contact with the father of the baby and without the support of a family or wider social network. The overall picture then is not at all favourable for a good start to life. Basically, the scenario shows the infant making demands upon the mother for nurture and security and the mother being unwilling and unable to meet these demands. The baby feels anxious and uncontained, becoming fretful and ever more demanding – only to find the mother unresponsive and impatient. As the child becomes a toddler, so he becomes more mobile, restless and increasingly demanding – seeking desperately the security and acknowledgement of his mother. The mother, however, experiences his behaviour as overwhelming: she feels she cannot cope and she becomes punitive and rejecting. The child now has two 'choices': either to demand more to claim his rightful place in his mother's life; or to give up and withdraw and become more 'independent'. The chances are that the mother, unless she can find support for herself, won't be able to gather enough energy to respond adequately – and her sense of failure, humiliation and shame in being a 'bad' mother may lead her to be ever more punitive and rejecting. The baby ends up feeling insecure and unloved. It has been an unhappy interplay. And now he is 'ready' for school.

Second scenario

The diagram facing, *Unhappy interplay at school,* illustrates the continuation of a difficult attachment between mother and child into the relationship between teacher and pupil:

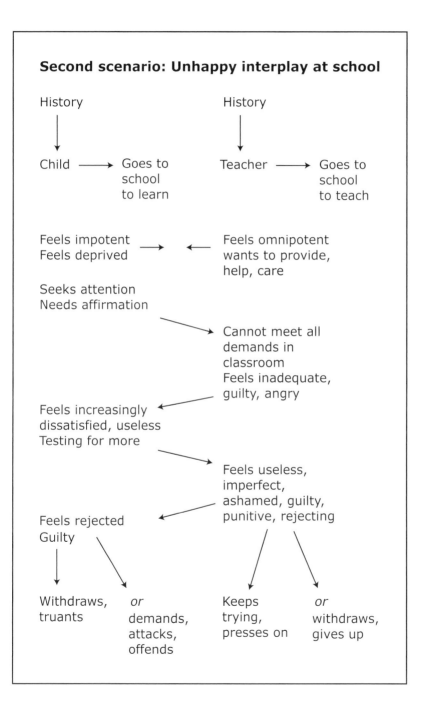

Second scenario: Unhappy interplay at school

History   History

Child ⟶ Goes to   Teacher ⟶ Goes to
             school   school
             to learn   to teach

Feels impotent ⟶   ⟵ Feels omnipotent
Feels deprived   wants to provide,
                               help, care

Seeks attention
Needs affirmation

                          Cannot meet all
                          demands in
                          classroom
                          Feels inadequate,
Feels increasingly   guilty, angry
dissatisfied, useless
Testing for more

                          Feels useless,
                          imperfect,
                          ashamed, guilty,
Feels rejected   punitive, rejecting
Guilty

Withdraws,   *or*   Keeps   *or*
truants   demands,   trying,   withdraws,
             attacks,   presses on   gives up
             offends

The second scenario gives a picture of what may occur in the classroom arising from the first scenario. The interplay is really determined by the histories of pupils and teachers and how they meet. In this case, we know of the child's history and we take it that he has come to school to learn. We don't know the story of the teacher's life but we do know that he has come to school to teach. A promising start for a dance. However, because of what has gone on earlier, the interplay soon gets

into difficulties. The child brings to school his experiences of rejection and deprivation and a sense of himself as a failure. He comes to school with the hope that he might find a more interested response from his teacher; yet, at the same time, he anticipates that he will receive the same kind of response he has been used to at home. He seeks attention and admiration. He may look for special privileges, he may become very clingy. He may expect the teacher to magically understand exactly what he wants. At first, the teacher is delighted to meet the child – a child who is in need, who is seeking a relationship. The teacher is moved to meet this challenge, to perhaps make up for what has not been accomplished so far. The child's sense of impotence is met by the teacher's sense of omnipotence – that is to say, a healthy omnipotence, a readiness to overcome difficulties and to provide all that is needed. In the beginning there is something of a hopeful match, a potential for a lively dance. The child, however, his needs having been so unmet in earlier life, becomes overly demanding. He constantly wants more, more than any mortal teacher can provide. The teacher wanes. He finds himself unable to provide enough to give the undivided attention the child seeks – particularly in the midst of a class of 30 other children, many with similar needs. The teacher begins to feel inadequate – and the child senses this and becomes ever more desperate. His behaviour becomes more fidgety, disruptive – anything to test the teacher to grab his attention, to have the teacher for himself. Unhappily a gradual disenchantment forms between the two of them – the one feeling so useless, the other a failure. The dance becomes jagged, disjointed, almost coming to a halt – ever more fuelled by anger, disappointment, rejection and counter-rejection. The teacher now feels powerless and guilty that he cannot live up to the initial promise. The danger is that he will find a way to withdraw or become punitive and retaliate. He may be dismissive, overly critical or sarcastic. At worst he may want to exclude the pupil from class. The child ends up feeling confirmed in all of his views about himself and in all the fears of what might happen. He feels unwanted, persecuted and a failure. He might give up and not come to school or he might fight back in protest – a recipe for challenging behaviour. The teacher has the choice, the task, with insight and support to keep trying, to not give up.

There are many other patterns of relationships that have their roots in early experience. They are not so much to do with difficulties of attachment as to do with particular kinds of experience that have left their mark in children's minds and on their development. The impact of these experiences on pupils' and teachers' ways of relating at school is considerable and places different emotional pressures on the teachers.

To illustrate something of this impact, we can imagine various examples in which children are in effect saying different kinds of hellos – that is, greetings that carry with them different kinds of anticipation of what might happen in new relationships.

Hellos from pupils

Hello, my dad hits me

Let's take, for example, a small child aged five, whose father has physically abused him a great deal during his childhood. He might come to school and say in effect:

> *Hello.*
> *My dad hits me.*
> *I don't know why.*
> *I'm afraid of him and angry.*
> *I feel bad.*
> *Now when I meet you (a man), I fear that you will hit me.*
> *That you will think I'm bad.*
> *I don't know what to expect but I wouldn't be surprised if you hit me.*
> *I just know you think I'm no good.*
> *I might even get you to hit me because that is what I'm used to. That way, I feel less scared because I'll know where I stand.*
> *But I don't like the way things are and I'm always terrified.*

*So I might just go away, I might just not turn up at school.
I don't care.
Or I might turn the tables on you.
I might frighten you, and make you feel bad and not know
what is going to happen next.
That way, you can feel all the bad things I feel and I can feel
strong.*

Hello, my mum didn't love me

Another example – an eight year old who has been neglected
and undernourished. This child might come to school and say
in effect:

*Hello.
My mum didn't love me and never used to feed me properly.
I felt sad and angry that she never cared about me.
I felt bad and worthless.
Now when I meet you (a woman), I expect you won't care
about me, you won't give me anything because that is what
I'm used to.
I just know you don't care about me.
I might even get you to ignore me.
I'll stay away from you or do something bad to see if you
care.
But I don't like the way things are and I always feel sad and
empty and useless.
So I might just give up, not turn up at school.
Take some drugs and have some fun.
Or I might turn the tables on you and pay no attention to
you.
And make you feel as stupid as I do.
That way you can feel unloved and unwanted as I do and
then I will be in charge.*

Hello, my dad puts me down

Another example, a 13 year old who is being emotionally
abused at home. This teenager might come to school and say
in effect:

Hello.
My dad is horrible to me.
He puts me down and then ignores me.
He laughs at me, at my clothes and says I'm rubbish.
I feel frightened and humiliated.
I feel bad and stupid.
I feel guilty. It must be my fault. I feel confused.
Now, when I meet you, I expect you to laugh at me the same way as he does because that's what happens.
I think you think I'm rubbish.
I might even provoke you to do something to take the piss out of me.
That way, I'll know where I am and anyway, that is what I'm used to.
But I don't like the way things are because it's not right and I feel hopeless and scared.
So I might just give in, who cares – let him say what he wants. He's my dad and I can't do anything.
Or I might go away. Leave school. Run away.
Don't get near me. Don't tease me or I might turn the tables on you.
And make you feel scared and little.
I might call you names and make you feel embarrassed.
I'll make you feel as abused and humiliated as I do.
That way I can make you feel how awful I feel – and I can be in control.

These are all very sad hellos. They are messages that rarely get spelt out in so many words. Instead they are conveyed more in the way pupils behave and approach teachers. They express the undercurrents of pupils' expectations. They do not predict what will happen in a new relationship – but what might happen, particularly if teachers are not aware and are unable to find more positive responses to counteract these negative thoughts and feelings. These hellos can of course be much more complicated – but the overall impact is invariably very disturbing and upsetting for teachers and for the pupils themselves.

All of these pupils are saying in effect that they cannot feel safe with anyone including the teachers. They cannot trust and they feel bad. How are teachers to respond? In their hellos, the pupils convey their expectations and even invitations to the teacher to behave in the same way they have come to expect. Teachers feel this pressure and find themselves feeling attacked, neglected, frightened, controlled, angry, guilty, and uncomfortable. They may well feel at times confused and mis-understood – and their confidence in themselves as teachers and as men and women undermined.

It has to be said that these feelings do not prevail all the time. They can be offset in so many ways by positive class-room management in a healthy school environment. Much depends, too, on the composition of the classroom. In some schools, there may be many children with difficult experiences such as these, leading to whole classes becoming over-whelmed by such conflicting and disturbing emotional demands. But it may well be in many other schools that there is a greater proportion of less troubled children, whose resilience and enjoyment of life adds strength to the whole class, to the teachers and other pupils.

Hello, my mum and dad love me

Lets take one more example – a 14 year old girl who has enjoyed from early on in her family life, securely attached rela-tionships:

> *Hello.*
> *I have felt loved by my mum and dad.*
> *I have felt secure.*
> *I feel good and worthwhile.*
> *I expect you to like me. I like you.*
> *I'm not afraid.*
> *I trust you and I want to learn from you.*
> *I want to be here.*
> *I want you to feel as loved as I feel.*

Simple, idyllic, too good to be true? Maybe. But the simplicity of this hello makes its point – and teachers feel appreciated and want to teach. A spirited dance; a lively interplay.

Teachers in the public eye

Teachers may be very knowledgeable about their subjects, they may be well resourced with all the necessary learning techniques and audio-visual aids – but what stands out above all else is their capacity to really care about the pupils in front of them and respond appropriately to their various demands. In the end what matters is how teachers can create a sense of order and reliability in the classroom. In many respects, process is more important than content. So much depends on how teachers go about their daily life – how they feel about themselves in front of their pupils. No matter how important friends may be to young people, teachers nevertheless stand out as a central point of reference, a model or guide as to how to be an adult. Many questioning eyes rest upon them.

This of course is not always the most comfortable position for anyone to be in, to be so very much in the public eye, without much of a hiding place. Some teachers cope with this well enough and even thrive on the drama of it all. Other teachers are less well at ease, more comfortable working within the curriculum of their particular subject. Most teachers, however, try to find ways of moving beyond their subject matter and developing relationships with their pupils.

In the middle of the busy life of the school and at the centre of so much interplay, it is inevitable that teachers will go through a whole range of feelings as they respond to the different ways that pupils feel and behave. They may be puzzled, unsure of themselves and surprised. They may not know what to make of the feelings aroused in them or what is the best thing to do. They may feel useless, even though they are managing well enough. There is nothing wrong or unusual about any of this. It is all to do with being part of the dynamic interplay, the dance of many pupils and teachers in a group situation.

But what really does count is that teachers find time to think about themselves in their work and in their relationships. Teachers need to find ways of keeping themselves aware and alert to what is going on within themselves, pupils and the whole situation. This is essential if teachers are to keep open to the learning possibilities and abilities of their pupils, and to

And what of the teachers?

not function out of weariness and exasperation. Ultimately it is the responsibility of the school management to ensure that time is given for this support.

References
1. With thanks to Jeanni Barlow who compiled this list. Jeanni Barlow is a freelance educational consultant and trainer and is an adviser on the YoungMinds Parents' Information Service.
2. This diagram has been adapted from: Fonagy, P. (1998). Prevention; the appropriate target of infant psychotherapy. *Infant Mental Health Journal*, vol 19 (2), pp 124-150.

Chapter 4

Schools that mind:
a summary and a plea
for teacher support

This book has stressed the importance of our schools for developing the minds of our young. It highlights the value of schools creating their own coherent cultures and policies, which involve everybody, affecting the whole school. It recognises the value of their academic achievements as well as their attention to emotional literacy and intelligence. It gives an account of the complexity and diversity of the development of young minds and the challenges that face teachers in understanding children's behaviour and finding the best ways of stimulating and encouraging learning.

Above all, it values the role of teachers in educating all children, and understanding and helping those with learning difficulties and those who are more troubled and disturbed, with emotional and behavioural problems or mental health problems.

Schools play a vital role in the promotion of children's mental health. There is much to be accomplished in creating healthy cultures in which there is time for children and staff to talk about what they are doing and to improve their relationships and learning. Schools are having to struggle with a constant tension between meeting the drive for achievement of high academic standards and outcomes, and yet respecting the concern for those who are less able to achieve in this way and who may be vulnerable or troublesome. Much depends on the commitment of senior management in schools together with all staff to sustain a balance between academic and emotional literacy in the school culture.

Much more depends on how schools support their teachers. It is essential that schools recognise that teachers need a wide range of practical, emotional and social support. It is very important that teachers' needs are addressed in a similar way to the pupils' needs. Teachers cannot carry out their work and stimulate the learning process if their own well-being is neglected. They need opportunities to stand back from the intensity of the classroom and to share their experiences; to learn from each other about their responses to the pupils and the solutions that they have found. Faced with the many difficulties encountered in their work, they need to remind themselves that there is rarely any one right response which a teacher can adopt in any given situation. They need to feel it is okay to make mistakes and to have all kinds of feelings, and to understand better the impact their pupils have on them as people. They need to be aware of the pressures that they are living with, to know better what they are in the midst of emotionally with their pupils, and to know what is reasonable for them to be able to do and not to do in their role as teachers.

This kind of thinking and reflection can well be arranged in various staff groups – either arranged on a self-help basis, or, ideally, with the facilitation of an external consultant. Of the greatest importance is that teachers are not left alone and isolated in their work. They need the chance to develop a relatively balanced attitude to their work, which ultimately is based on their own self-awareness. For this to be accomplished, it is imperative that a culture of support generally exists in the school as a whole in which teachers can be encouraged to explore and learn from their doubts and uncertainties about their work without fear of rebuke, censure or accusation of incompetence.

APPENDICES

1. Some basic facts about children's mental health

All children have their ups and downs and go through a range of emotions as they grow up. With the back-up of those around them, most children cope well enough. Some, however, don't do so well. Without the right conditions and support, problems may arise which can have a significant effect on a young person's future and can lead to some serious difficulties in later life. Children can become unhappy at school and refuse to attend; they can have difficulty concentrating; they can get into trouble, or have eating or sleeping problems. These are problems that affect children's well-being. In schools they are usually called emotional and behavioural problems. In health agencies they are referred to as mental health problems or disorders. Social workers may refer to children as being 'at risk' or 'in need'.

The extent of such problems varies. Some are transitory and are called mild and moderate. Others persist to the point where children become distressed, confused or out of control, and when families feel they cannot manage. When these problems become severe and significantly interfere with everyday functioning and general development, child and adolescent mental health specialists call them mental disorders.

Prevalence of disorders

In 2000 a national survey of 10,438 children and their families[1] showed that in Great Britain 10% or 1 in 10 children and young people aged 5-15 and living in private households, had a diagnosable mental disorder. This figure is likely to be even higher in urban areas. According to the 2001 Census, there are about 10 million children under 15 in Great Britain[2], so this means that almost 1 million will have a mental disorder.

In a primary school with 250 pupils approximately 20 children will have a significant mental disorder[1]:

- 7 children will have an anxiety disorder (4 of these children will be affected by phobias)
- 1 will be seriously depressed
- 12 will have a conduct disorder
- 4 will have hyperkinetic disorder or severe ADHD

Some of these conditions affect boys more than girls. Boys are much more likely to have a conduct disorder or hyperkinetic disorder. Some children will have more than one disorder.

In a secondary school with 1,000 pupils approximately 112 children will have a significant mental disorder[1]:

- 46 will have an anxiety disorder (15 of these children will be affected by phobias)
- 18 will be seriously depressed
- 62 will have a conduct disorder
- 14 will have hyperkinetic disorder or severe ADHD

Again, boys are more likely to have a conduct disorder or hyperkinetic disorder, and girls are more likely to have an anxiety disorder, and some children will have more than one disorder.

Vulnerable groups

In some vulnerable groups, the prevalence of mental disorders is even higher. One such group is young people in local authority care. A study found that 45% of young people aged 5-17 looked after by local authorities had a mental disorder, and some of them suffered from more than one disorder. Thirty-seven per cent had clinically significant conduct disorders, 12% were assessed as having emotional disorders and 7% were rated as hyperactive[3]. Refugee and asylum-seeking children[4], as well as children whose parents have mental health problems[5], also have higher levels of mental disorders.

Eating disorders

Both girls and boys can develop eating disorders. It is far more common in girls and young women. The age for on-set is between 15-25 years[6]. The survey carried out by Meltzer et al[1] found that amongst 11-15 year-olds, 0.4% of girls and 0.1% of boys had a serious eating disorder.

Self-harm

A survey carried out on behalf of Samaritans, found that 10% of 15-16 year-olds have self-harmed. Girls are much more likely to self-harm than boys. The research found that 11% of girls, compared to 3.2% of boys self-harmed[7].

Bullying

The Department for Education and Skills' (DfES) anti-bullying pack refers to studies showing that bullying is widespread across primary and secondary schools[8]. A recent report commissioned by ChildLine and DfES, found that over a half of all primary and secondary school pupils thought that bullying was a big problem in their school. Just over a half of year 5 pupils, and about a quarter of year 8 pupils had been bullied during that school term[9].

Research shows that bullying can have a detrimental impact on mental health. A survey carried out by Young Voice, found that boys who were victimised had much higher levels of depression at age 23[10].

References

1. Meltzer, H. et al. (2000). *The Mental health of children and adolescents in Great Britain*. London: Stationery Office. Statistics were used from this report to estimate the prevalence of overall and specific mental health disorders.
2. Office for National Statistics (2003). *Census 2001: Population Statistics – United Kingdom*. URL: http://www.statistics.gov.uk/census2001
3. Meltzer, H. et al. (2003). *The mental health of young people looked after by local authorities in England*. Page xii. London: Stationery Office.
4. Woodcock, J. (2003). Practical approaches to work with refugee children. In Dwivedi, K. N. (ed). *Meeting the needs of ethnic minority Children*. Chapter 13. London: Jessica Kingsley.
5. Aldridge, J. & Becker, S. (2003). *Children caring for parents with mental illness*. Bristol: Policy Press.
6. Eating Disorders Association. *What is an eating disorder?* Norwich: EDA. URL: http://www.edauk.com/what_is_eating_disorder.htm
7. Centre for Suicide Research (2003). *Youth and self-harm: perspectives*. Page 2. Ewell, Surrey: Samaritans. URL: http://www.samaritans.org/know/selfharm/aboutselfharm.shtm
8. Department for Education and Skills (2002). *Bullying: don't suffer in silence – an anti-bullying pack for schools*. London: Department for Education and Skills. URL: http://www.dfes.gov.uk/bullying/pack/02.pdf
9. Oliver, C. & Candappa, M. (2003). *Tackling bullying: listening to the views of children and young people*. London: Department for Education and Skills. URL: http://www.dfes.gov.uk/research/data/uploadfiles/RR400.pdf
10. Katz, A. et al. (2001). *Bullying in Britain: testimonies from teenagers*. East Molesey, Surrey: Young Voice.

2. Who else can help?

There are a wide variety of organisations that can provide help and support:

ACE (Advisory Centre for Education)
1c Aberdeen Studios
22 Highbury Grove
London N5 2DQ
Tel: 020 7354 8318
Advice line: 0808 800 5793
Exclusion help-line: 020 7704 9822
Email: enquiries@ace.dialnet.com
Website: www.ace-ed.org
Advice and information particularly about special needs, school exclusions, admissions and bullying.

ADDISS (The National Attention Deficit Disorder Information and Support Service)
PO BOX 340
Edgware
Middlesex HA8 9HL
Tel: 020 8906 9068
Email: info@addiss.co.uk
Website: www.addiss.co.uk
National organisation providing information and support to parents, teachers and others regarding Attention Deficit Disorder.

The Anti-Bullying Campaign
185 Tower Bridge Road
London SE1 2UF
Tel: 020 7378 1446
Offers information and support to school children who are being bullied and to adults wanting advice.

Antidote (Campaign for Emotional Literacy)
3rd floor Cityside House
Adler Street
Aldgate
London E1 1EE
Tel: 020 7247 3355
Website: www.antidote.org.uk
Antidote's aim is to try and help to create an emotionally liter-ate culture. It is working to establish emotional literacy in schools and other organisations.

The Caspari Foundation (for educational therapy and thera-peutic teaching)
Caspari House
1 Noel Road
The Angel
Islington
London N1 8HQ
Tel: 020 7704 1977
Email: admin@caspari.org.uk
Website: www.caspari.org.uk
An organisation concerned with the role of the emotions in education and how to help children who have difficulty in learning.

The Child Psychotherapy Trust
Star House
104-108 Grafton Road
London NW5 4BD
Tel: 020 7284 1355
Email: cpt@globalnet.co.uk
Website: www.childpsychotherapytrust.org.uk
Promotes understanding of child and adolescent development and psychotherapeutic approaches to problems.

The Children's Society
Edward Rudolph House
Margery Street
London WC1X 0JL
Tel: 020 7841 4400
Website: www.the-childrens-society.org.uk
A society that is committed to helping disadvantaged young people.

Cruse Bereavement Care
Cruse House
126 Sheen Road
Richmond
Surrey TW9 1UR
Helpline: 0870 167 1677
Helpline for young people aged 12-18: 0808 808 1677
Email helpline: helpline@crusebereavementcare.org.uk
Website: www.crusebereavementcare.org.uk
Offers help to anyone suffering bereavement including young people.

Depression Alliance
35 Westminster Bridge Road
London SE1 7JB
Tel: 020 7633 0557
Email: information@depressionalliance.org.uk
Website: www.depressionalliance.org.uk
Provides information and support for people affected by depression.

Eating Disorders Association
103 Prince of Wales Road
Norwich NR1 1DW
Adult helpline: 0845 634 1414
Youth helpline: 0845 634 7650
Textphone: 01603 753 322
Email: helpmail@edauk.com
Website: www.edauk.com
Promotes understanding of eating disorders and provides a national network of self-help groups.

Kidscape
2 Grosvenor Gardens
London SW1W 0DH
Tel: 020 7730 3300
Website: www.kidscape.org.uk
Provides support and information for students and offers counselling for parents and training for schools.

Mediation UK
Alexander House
Telephone Avenue
Bristol BS1 4BS
Tel: 0117 904 6661
Email: enquiry@mediationuk.org.uk
Website: www.mediationuk.org.uk
An umbrella organisation concerned with organisations, projects and individuals involved in community mediation and conflict resolution.

Mental Health Foundation
83 Victoria Street
London SW1H 0HW
Tel: 020 7802 0300
Email: mhf@mhf.org.uk
Website: www.mentalhealth.org.uk
A national foundation that aims to improve mental health services. Has useful publications and conferences.

Mind (the national association for mental health)
15-19 Broadway
London E15 4BQ
Tel: 020 8519 2122
Information line: 0845 766 2122
Email: contact@mind.org.uk
Website: www.mind.org.uk
Provides support and information concerning mental health.

NASEN (National Association for Special Educational Needs)
Nasen House
4-5 Amber Business Village
Amber Close
Amington
Tamworth B77 4RP
Tel: 01827 311 500
Email: via website
Website: www.nasen.org.uk
A body of teachers and others concerned with the welfare and education of children with special needs.

The National Pyramid Trust
84 Uxbridge Road
London W13 8RA
Tel: 020 8579 5108
Email: enquiries@nptrust.org.uk
Website: www.nptrust.org.uk
An organisation that helps students to fulfil their potential and emphasises early interventions and multi-disciplinary approaches. Promotes 'Pyramid Clubs' to identify and support vulnerable students.

The National Self Harm Network
PO BOX 7264
Nottingham NG1 6WJ
Email: info@nshn.co.uk
Website: www.nshn.co.uk
A survivor led campaign organisation.

SAMH (Scottish Association for Mental Health)
Cumbrae House
15 Carlton Court
Glasgow G5 9JP
Tel: 0141 568 7000
Email: enquire@samh.org.uk
Website: www.samh.org.uk
Provides support and information concerning mental health.

School Councils UK
Lawford House
5 Albert Place
London N3 1QB
Tel: 020 8349 2459
Email: info@schoolcouncils.org.uk
Website: www.schoolcouncils.org.uk
Provides training and support so that schools can set up school councils and also offers help with student behaviour charters, peer mediation, buddying and circle time.

SEBDA (Social, Emotional and Behavioural Difficulties Association)
Church House
1 St Andrew's View
Penrith
Cumbria CA10 7YF
Tel: 01768 210510
Email: admin@sebda.org
Website: www.sebda.co.uk
This is a multi-disciplinary association that exists to represent the interests of children displaying emotional and behavioural difficulties. It helps to promote sharing and communication between all professionals working to support these young people.

Self Esteem Network
32 Carisbrooke Road
Walthamstow
London E17 7EF
Promotes the importance of raising self-esteem.

Teacher Support Network
Helpline: 08000 562 561
Websites: www.teacherline.org.uk and www.worklifesupport.com
A support, counselling and signposting service for teachers. Offers support and seminars to promote teacher health and well-being.

Winston's Wish
Helpline: 0845 2030405
Email: info@winstonswish.org.uk
Website: www.winstonswish.org.uk
A grief support service for bereaved children.

YoungMinds
102-108 Clerkenwell Road
London EC1M 5SA
Tel: 020 7336 8445
Parents' Information Service: 0800 018 2138
Email: enquiries@youngminds.org.uk
Website: www.youngminds.org.uk
YoungMinds is the national charity committed to improving the mental health of all babies, children and young people. YoungMinds Parents' Information Service is a free confidential telephone service providing information and advice to any adult with concerns about the mental health of a child or young person.

3. Further reading

Aldridge, J. & Becker, S. (2003). *Children caring for parents with mental illness.* Bristol: Policy Press.

Alexander, T. (2002). *Bright futures for all: promoting mental health in education.* London: Mental Health Foundation.

Atkinson, M. & Hornby, G. (2002). *Mental health handbook for schools.* London: Routledge.

Barrett, M. & Trevitt, J. (1991). *Attachment behaviour and the school child.* London: Routledge.

Bennathan, M. & Boxall, M. (1996). *Effective intervention in primary schools: nurture groups.* London: David Fulton Publishers.

Centre for Suicide Research (2003). *Youth and self-harm: perspectives.* Page 2. Ewell, Surrey: Samaritans. URL: http://www.samaritans.org/know/selfharm/aboutselfharm.shtm

Cowie, H. & Sharp, S. (eds.) (1996). *Peer counselling in schools: a time to listen.* London: David Fulton Publishers.

Crittenden, P.M. & Clausen, A.H. (eds.) (2000). *The Organisation of Attachment Relationships: Maturation, Culture and Context.* Cambridge: Cambridge University Press.

Department for Education and Department of Health (1994). *The Education of Children with Emotional and Behavioural Difficulties.* DFE 9/94: DH LAC (94) 9. London: Department for Education.

Department for Education and Skills (2001). *Promoting children's mental health within early years and school settings.* London: Department for Education and Skills. URL: http://www.dfes.gov.uk/mentalhealth/index.shtml

Department for Education and Skills (2002). *Bullying: don't suffer in silence – an anti-bullying pack for schools.* London: Department for Education and Skills. URL: http://www.dfes.gov.uk/bullying/pack/02.pdf

Department for Education and Skills (2002). *Intervening early: a snapshot of approaches primary schools can use to help children get the best from school.* London: Department for Education and Skills. URL: http://www.dfes.gov.uk/sen/documents/Intervening_Early.pdf

Eating Disorders Association. *What is an eating disorder?* Norwich: EDA. URL: http://www.edauk.com/what_is_eating_disorder.htm

Elias, M. et al. (1997). *Promoting social and emotional learning.* Alexandria, VA: Association for Supervision and Curriculum Development (ASCD).

Feinstein, L. (2001). *The relative economic importance of academic, psychological and behavioural attributes developed in childhood.* Presented to Institute for Public Policy Research seminar on Mainstreaming Mental Health in Schools, London, 2 March 2001.

Fonagy, P., Target, M., Steele, H., Leigh, T., Levinson, A., & Kennedy, R. (1997). Morality, disruptive behaviour, borderline personality disorder, crime, and their relationships to security of attachment. In Atkinson, L. & Zucker, K.J. (eds.), *Attachment and psychopathology.* New York: Guildford Press.

Goleman, D. (1996). *Emotional intelligence: why it can matter more than IQ.* London: Bloomsbury.

Graham, P. & Hughes, C. (1995). *So young, so sad, so listen.* London: Gaskell.

Greenhalgh, P. (1994). *Emotional growth and learning.* London: Routledge.

Hanko, G. (1999). *Increasing competence through collaborative problem solving: using insight into social and emotional factors in children's learning.* London: David Fulton Publishers.

Hornby, G., Davis, G., Taylor, G. (1995). *The special educational needs co-ordinators handbook.* London: Routledge.

Jackson, E. (2002). Mental health in schools: what about the staff? *Journal of Child Psychotherapy*, vol 28 (2), pp. 129-146.

Katz, A. et al. (2001). *Bullying in Britain: testimonies from teenagers.* East Molesey, Surrey: Young Voice.

Maehr, M. & Midgely, C. (1996). *Transforming school cultures.* Boulder, CO: Westview Press.

Meltzer, H. et al. (2000). *The Mental health of children and adolescents in Great Britain.* London: Stationery Office.

Meltzer, H. et al. (2003). *The mental health of young people looked after by local authorities in England.* London: Stationery Office.

Mental Health Foundation (1999). *Bright futures: promoting children and young people's mental health.* London: Mental Health Foundation.

Mosley, J. (1993). *Turn your school around.* Wisbech: LDA.

Murray, L. & Andrews, L. (2000). *The social baby: understanding babies' communication from birth*. Richmond, Surrey: CP Publishing.

Office for National Statistics (2003). *Census 2001: Population Statistics-United Kingdom.* URL: http://www.statistics.gov.uk/census2001

Oliver, C. & Candappa, M. (2003). *Tackling bullying: listening to the views of children and young people.* London: Department for Education and Skills. URL: http://www.dfes.gov.uk/research/data/uploadfiles/RR400.pdf

Reid, K. (1989). Bullying and persistent school absenteeism. In Tattum, D. & Lane, D. (1989). *Bullying in schools.* Stoke on Trent: Trentham.

Sharp, S. & Cowie, H. (1998). C*ounselling and supporting children in distress.* London: Sage.

Sroufe, L.A. (1998). *Emotional Development.* Cambridge: Cambridge University Press.

Stacey, H. & Robinson, P. (1997). *Let's mediate: a teachers' guide to peer support and conflict resolution skills for all ages.* Bristol: Lucky Duck.

Weare, K. (2000). *Promoting mental, emotional and social health: a whole school approach.* London: Routledge.

Wilson, P. & Bottomley, V. (1980). The emotional climate in the classroom: the interaction between adult teacher and early adolescent student. In Upton, G. & Gobell, A. (eds.) (1980). *Behaviour problems in the comprehensive school*. Cardiff: Faculty of Education, University College Cardiff.

Winkley, L. (1999). Neural pathways and the development of the brain. *Primary Practice,* No. 20, pp. 30-35.

Woodcock, J. (2003). Practical approaches to work with refugee children. In Dwivedi, K. N. (ed). *Meeting the needs of ethnic minority Children.* Chapter 13. London: Jessica Kingsley.

4. YoungMinds Publications

YoungMinds has developed a range of publications which address the mental health problems affecting young people. These include:

Booklets for young people

This is a range of colourful, pocket sized (A6) booklets for 11-16 year-olds which offer them information, advice and details of useful organisations that they can contact for further support. Many young people have found these booklets helpful. One 13 year old girl said that the: 'booklets will come in handy in primary and secondary schools all over the country, because I'm only 13 and I know quite a lot of people in my year group who are having a hard time at the moment and would find these booklets very useful.'

The following booklets for young people are available:

- do you ever feel depressed?
- worried about self-injury?
- in school, stay cool (helps children cope with some of the problems they may encounter at school)
- mental illness in your family?
- sexually abused?
- feeling angry?
- adolescent in-patient units – need to know more?
- want to know more about psychosis?
- worried about eating problems and disorders?
- entering adulthood?

Information Leaflets

These leaflets aim to provide parents and professionals with straight-forward and factual information about mental health problems and the role of some of the services that may be able to help.

The following Information Leaflets are available:

- Why do young minds matter?
- Worried about a young person's eating problems?
- Children and young people get depressed too
- Bullying – why it matters
- What is Attention Deficit Hyperactivity Disorder?
- Do you know someone who has been sexually abused?
- What are Child and Adolescent Mental Health Services?

Signposts & Resources

These are A4 sheets about specific issues relating to children and their mental health. They include details of organisations which can offer advice, information or counselling; and details of books, leaflets and tapes etc. which can offer more support and information.

Signposts & Resources are available on the following topics:

- Children under 12
- Adolescents
- ADHD
- Depression
- Anxiety and obsessions
- Education
- Eating problems
- Self-Injury
- Mental health problems
- Bereavement
- Divorce and separation
- Child abuse
- Legal and advocacy
- Adoption
- Living away from home
- Violence in the home

YoungMinds Guides

This range of A5 booklets for parents and professionals provides factual information on key issues and answers questions often asked about how change will affect children:

- Tuning in to our babies – examines the importance of the parent/baby relationship
- Keeping in touch – emphasises the importance of both parents maintaining contact with their children after separation or divorce

Other Publications

- Directory of Child & Adolescent Mental Health Services
- The Wise Mouse (a book for children on parental mental illness)
- So many feelings… (explores some of the feelings teenagers may experience)

YoungMinds is continually expanding its range of publications. For more information about any of these publications or to obtain a full list of publications and an order form, please visit www.youngminds.org.uk/publications or call YoungMinds on 020 7336 8445.

About YoungMinds

YoungMinds is the national charity committed to promoting and improving the mental health of all babies, children and young people. This aim underpins all of YoungMinds services.

The national telephone helpline, YoungMinds Parents' Information Service, provides information and advice for any adult with concerns about the mental health of a child or young person. The service is free and confidential and takes thousands of calls from parents, carers, and professionals such as teachers and counsellors worried about a particular child or young person. Many of YoungMinds publications address issues raised by callers to YoungMinds Parents' Information Service (see appendix 4).

YoungMinds campaigns about the importance of children's mental health; the importance of recognising when a child is troubled and of providing adequate support for these children before their problems escalate out of control. Through lobbying, press releases, research and policy documents, YoungMinds has become increasingly influential in driving for changes and improvements in services for children and young people.

The Consultancy and Training Service helps to support managers and practitioners in the field of child and adolescent mental health and to develop and implement these changes and improvements.

YoungMinds also publishes YoungMinds Magazine, a bi-monthly magazine for everyone who works with children and young people. It is a leading source of up to date news and features on a wide range of issues affecting children's lives.

To obtain further copies of this book (ref YMS), contact YoungMinds.

YoungMinds
102-108 Clerkenwell Road, London EC1M 5SA
Tel: 020 7336 8445
Fax: 020 7336 8446
Email: enquiries@youngminds.org.uk
Website: www.youngminds.org.uk
Parents' Information Service: 0800 018 2138

Registered Charity no. 1016968

Freephone supplied by MCI WorldCom

About the author

Peter Wilson has been Director of YoungMinds for over 12 years. He began professional life as an unattached youth worker. He qualified as a social worker at the London School of Economics and Political Science in the 1960s and as a Child Psychoanalyst at the Anna Freud Centre in the 1970s. He lived in New York and London and worked in a variety of child guidance centres and adolescent services for many years. In the 1980s he was the Director of the Brandon Centre, an adolescent counselling service, and was Senior Clinical Tutor at the Institute of Psychiatry. He was also Consultant Psychotherapist at Peper Harow therapeutic community for disturbed adolescents in Surrey. Throughout this time he has spent a great deal of time with teachers and other professionals, providing consultation in different settings. In his role as Director of YoungMinds, he has campaigned in various ways to raise public awareness of the importance of the mental health of children.

He is married, with three grown up children and one of his greatest pleasures is playing jazz piano.